Business Rule Concepts

Third Edition

Getting to the Point of Knowledge

by Ronald G. Ross

Co-Founder and Principal, Business Rule Solutions, LLC
Executive Editor, BRCommunity.com
Chair, Business Rules Forum Conference

D1341562

 Business Rule Solu...   RCommunity.com

Business Rule Concepts
Getting to the Point of Knowledge

Third Edition

by Ronald G. Ross

10 9 8 7 6 5 4 3 2 1

ISBN 0-941049-07-8

To Vanessa

Acknowledgments

My thanks to Gladys S.W. Lam for making this third edition of *Business Rule Concepts* possible. Gladys is my partner and co-founder of Business Rule Solutions, LLC, and the source of many (or most) of the practical ideas in Proteus®, our methodology for business analysis and business rule capture and management. Gladys is also Executive Director of the Business Rules Forum Conference and Publisher of BRCommunity.com.

I would also like to thank Keri Anderson Healy, Editor of the *Business Rules Journal*, BRCommunity.com, for her editorial assistance and her many suggestions for clarifying and enhancing the content. She did that for the first-edition drafts of the material and then, unbelievably, seven years later went through the whole process yet again for the second edition. Now, even more unbelievably, she's gone through the whole process yet again four years later for this third edition.

In addition, I would like to thank Daniel Berry, University of Waterloo, for his careful reading and many helpful suggestions included in this third edition.

Also, I am indebted to all the people who have worked so hard on SBVR, a landmark standard for business rules. (You know who you are.)

Finally, I would like to thank all the people who have helped make this book popular enough for a second, and then a third edition.

Contents

Preface

The Business Rules Paradigm

The Body Analogy

The human body is marvelous in many respects, not the least of which is its mechanics. Roughly, support for the mechanics of the human body has three basic components, separate yet intimately interconnected, as follows.

Structure is provided by the bones, which are organized and connected within the skeleton. The skeleton provides both a framework for carrying the weight of the other components as well as a semi-rigid scheme around which the other, softer components can be organized.

Power is provided through the muscles, which are connected to the bones. The muscles enable motion based on the framework provided by the skeleton. Since motion is what we see happening from outside the body, the muscles seem most directly responsible for the behavior we perceive.

Control is provided by the nervous system, which connects to the muscles. Nerves indirectly connect muscles to other muscles through long series of connections passing through the brain. Responses to all stimuli are coordinated through the firing of nerve impulses — no firing, no movement, and therefore no behavior.

These basic mechanical components are familiar to us all. In a moment, we will see how the mechanics of business operations should be viewed in the very same way. As we examine the analogy, several observations about the mechanics of the human body are worth keeping in mind.

- All three components are *essential*. The human body literally cannot function without all three.

- The three components are all interconnected — that is, they are *integrated* with each other. For example, tendons connect muscle to bone. Successful behavior depends on this integration.

- Each of the three components is *specialized* for a particular role or responsibility. Each optimizes for its particular task. Mixing or combining the three components would provide a much less effective solution. Also, specialization provides for greater simplicity. Think about how much more complex bones would be if they incorporated muscles or how much more complex muscles would be if they incorporated nerves.

- The nervous system in some sense is the most important component because it provides coordination and control for the other two. The body is certainly capable of behavior without a well-organized nervous system — but not *effective, adaptive* behavior. Literally, you cannot operate at your best with only half a brain!

The Organization of Business Operations

We believe that business operations should be organized in a manner similar to the mechanical system of the human body. Let's revisit the three components of that system, thinking now about business operations in place of the human body.

Structure

Structure is provided by organized — that is, *structured* — knowledge about basic things in the operational part of the business. Generally, this knowledge consists of two kinds:

- Everyday noun concepts — things we refer to with nouns.
- Everyday connections we make between those noun concepts — things we often say using verbs.

These 'basic things we can know' are often simply taken for granted — just like the human skeleton in everyday activity.

2

Think of the noun concepts as bones, and the verb-ish connections between them as ligaments (that is, bone-to-bone connections).

- Just as each bone has a particular shape that is optimal for its purpose and location, so too must each noun concept have a carefully-crafted 'shape'. A concept's shape is given by its definition, which must be clear, concise, and well-suited for its business purpose.

- Every bone or noun concept should also have a standard name. The standard name for a noun concept is a *term*.

- Each ligament also has a particular shape that is optimal for its purpose and location. Similarly, each verb-ish connection between noun concepts must also have a standard 'shape'. These shapes are expressed by *wordings* that reference the relevant terms.

Definitions, terms, and wordings are all about meaning, the stuff of *vocabularies*. Vocabularies represent what we know about the operational business and how we can talk about it in an organized fashion.

These days, discussion of vocabularies often falls under the heading *semantics*. Although it's fair to say this whole book is about semantics, I seldom use that term. It sounds arcane. I will generally just say *meaning* whenever the opportunity arises. There is really nothing arcane about the vocabulary of day-to-day business operations — no need for buzzwords or technical hype, just a lot of common sense.

A drawing or diagram of the complete human skeleton helps us understand how all the bones fit together. To illustrate overall vocabulary structure for a business at the operational level, it is likewise helpful to create a drawing or diagram. We call such a drawing a graphical *fact model*.

A fact model provides a framework, in many ways like a skeleton, in two basic respects.

1. A fact model literally provides a structure around which the other components can be organized — that is, the 'basic things we can know' *in common* about the business at the operational level.

2. A fact model bears the 'weight' of the organization — that is, its *collective* or *shared know-how*, as put to use by its processes and business rules.

Power

Power is provided by *processes*, which operate on the structure. Whereas the fact model provides for structure, the processes provide for activity.

When we think about a business, its processes are often the first things that come to mind. Processes literally *do* what the business needs to get done (e.g., take the customer's order). However, viewing business operations as merely a collection of processes makes no more sense than viewing the human body as merely a collection of muscles. Any organism is much more than that — whether human or business.

Control

Control is provided by *business rules*, which constrain processes (the 'muscles') to act only in certain ways deemed best for the business as a whole. In the human body, there are literally hundreds of muscles, which must act in concert. If they do not, the resulting behavior won't be optimal. At worst, serious damage can result (e.g., hyperextension of a limb) that will significantly reduce the body's overall capacity to act.

Similarly, business operations encompass dozens (or hundreds) of 'muscles' (processes), which must act in concert. If they do not, the resulting behavior won't be optimal either. In some cases, serious damage can result (e.g., loss of customers, squandering of resources or opportunities, and so on) that will significantly reduce the business's overall capacity to act (that is, its competitiveness or effectiveness).

In the human body, we take many control actions of the nervous system for granted. For example, who thinks about the impulses sent to the heart to make it beat — unless, of course, something goes wrong? Or who in saying "Ouch!" thinks much about the jerk reflex that causes the hand to move so quickly off the hot stove? So long as all runs smoothly, we can apply our mental faculties to a higher purpose — whether for strategic or tactical advantage, solving a problem, or simply planning a fun lunchtime getaway.

Similarly, while operations run smoothly in the business, we can take the control provided by the business rules for granted and concentrate on matters requiring a higher degree of intelligence. Until a business rule 'breaks' somehow — and that is a very important possibility, of course — we can focus on the more creative aspects of the business.

Summary

A business is very much like a human body — a living organism.

- Structure, the skeleton, is provided by basic noun concepts as represented by terms, and verb-ish connections between those noun concepts as represented by wordings.
- Power, the muscles, is provided by processes.
- Control and coordination, the nerves, are provided by business rules.

Let's revisit the observations I made earlier about the mechanics of the human body, now applying them to business operations.

- All three components — fact model, processes, and business rules — are *essential*. A business literally falls apart, disintegrates, without all three.
- The three components are obviously interrelated. For example, the processes act on knowledge about things represented in the fact model. These actions, in turn, are subject to the business rules. Successful business behavior depends on effective *integration*. These fundamental interrelationships must obviously be taken into account.
- Each of the three components is *specialized* for a particular role or responsibility and optimized for its particular task. Mixing or combining them would provide a less effective solution. Therefore the business rules need to be factored into a separate *rulebook* (automated, of course). We call this separation *Rule Independence*. As a fringe benefit comes a huge simplification in the processes. Indeed, now it is legitimate for the first time to talk of truly *thin* processes — a long-standing goal among many information technology (IT) professionals.
- In many ways business rules are the most important component since they provide control for the other two. The business and its systems are certainly capable of behavior without a well-organized set of business rules — but not *effective, adaptive* behavior. Literally, business rules are what make a business more than half-smart in how it operates.

These four observations represent the basic ideas of the *business rules paradigm*.

About this Book

This book is divided into four main parts.

Part 1: The Key Ideas

Part 1 is aimed toward the general reader seeking to understand the basic ideas of the business rules paradigm. It starts with business vocabulary, moves on to business rules, and concludes by discussing implications for the business manager or project leader. If you already have some knowledge of these things, or have read earlier editions of this book, you may find you can jump comfortably right into Parts 2–4.

Part 2: Business Vocabularies and Fact Models

Part 2 is all about business vocabularies and fact models — i.e., semantic structure. It discusses how to build a well-organized business vocabulary and to represent it as a graphical fact model. Fact models serve many important purposes other than simply design of data models or class diagrams, especially to express business rules, IT requirements, and other forms of business communication. So the discussion picks up with *verbalization*.

Part 3: Business Rules

Part 3 examines business rules in depth. The emphasis is on capture and communication of business rules in a form that is business-friendly yet robust. It explains the difference between business rules versus data or system rules. It also examines the surprising relationship between business rules and events. You will be guided through all the important things you need to know about business rules.

Part 4: Enterprise Design

Part 4 explores the role business rules play in smart architectures, smart knowledge management, smart (*simpler*) business processes, and smart (*really* smart) systems. It examines *point of knowledge*, a real place — the place where business rules happen. It explains how real-time compliance, continuous learning, and worker empowerment are a three-in-one solution. In closing, you are invited to probe the leading edge in achieving really thin, really agile, really dynamic processes.

About ...

Business Rules Manifesto — The *Manifesto* is a two-page, 2003 work product of the Business Rules Group (BRG), laying out the basic principles of the business rules paradigm. For easy reference, it is published as an Appendix to this book. The *Manifesto* has now been translated into more than a dozen languages. See www.BusinessRulesGroup.org.

SBVR — The formal basis for this book is given by *Semantics of Business Vocabularies and Business Rules* (SBVR), a standard officially released in December, 2007 by the Object Management Group (OMG). The treatment of business vocabulary and business rules in this book is based on, and entirely consistent with, SBVR. For background on SBVR, refer to [Ross 2008].

RuleSpeak® — All business rules in this book are expressed in RuleSpeak (unless noted otherwise). RuleSpeak is a business rule notation developed by Business Rule Solutions, LLC (BRS) for expressing business rules in structured natural language. It has been used directly with hundreds of business people in numerous large-scale projects beginning in the mid-1990s. RuleSpeak was one of three reference notations used in the creation of SBVR and is consistent with that standard. Basic RuleSpeak guidelines are available for free on www.RuleSpeak.com in English, Spanish, German, and Dutch, with other languages to follow.

MWUD — All natural-language definitions in this book, unless noted otherwise, are from *Merriam-Webster Unabridged Dictionary* (MWUD), Version 2.5, 2000. Any emphasis appearing in these definitions has been added.

Us — We (and 'our') as used in this book refers to Business Rule Solutions, LLC (BRS). The techniques we use for business rules are embodied in **Proteus**®, our methodology for business analysis and business rule capture and management. The graphical notation for fact models used in this book has been developed in large-scale client projects by BRS starting in the mid-1990s and is part of Proteus. It is consistent with, but not necessitated by, SBVR.

Part 1

The Key Ideas

Chapter 1

What You Need to Know About Structured Business Vocabularies

In the human body, structure is provided by the skeleton. The skeleton has two basic components: the bones and the ligaments that connect the bones. Even though the bones are larger and in a sense more basic, both components are essential.

In everyday business operations, structure is given by business vocabulary, or more precisely by the concepts represented in the vocabulary. There is a whole lot more to a vocabulary than you might imagine. Without any exaggeration, a good business vocabulary is no less important to effective business operation than a strong and complete skeleton is to the human body.

Like the skeleton for the human body, a business vocabulary likewise has two components: noun concepts as represented by *terms,* and verb-ish connections between those noun concepts as represented by *wordings.* These noun concepts and verb-ish connections are equivalent to bones and ligaments, respectively. They give structure to basic business knowledge — that is, they represent fundamental things in the operational business you need to know about. The terms and wordings given to them, in turn, let you talk about those things in a standard way.

We like to visualize this structure by means of a graphical fact model, representing the skeleton, or blueprint, for the basic knowledge needed in business operations. I will illustrate later.

> Noun concepts and verb-ish connections between them give structure to basic business knowledge. Terms and wordings let you talk about that knowledge in a standard way.

About Noun Concepts and Terms that Represent Them

A *term* is a noun or noun phrase that workers recognize and use in business communications of all kinds — for example, in agreements, procedure manuals, schedules, directives, training, instructions, and so on. Requirements for IT systems, and the documentation and help or guidance messages in operational IT systems, are additional forms of business communication.

A term carries a particular meaning for the business, which should be unambiguous given a particular context of usage. Some examples:

customer	employee name	date
prospect	delivery date due	high-risk customer
shipment	manager	employee
order	gender	line item
invoice	status	quantity back-ordered

Our meaning of *term* comes straight from *Webster's*. Note the key words *precisely limited meaning* in this definition.

Term: *a word or expression that has a precisely limited meaning in some uses or is peculiar to a science, art, profession, trade, or special subject*

Merriam-Webster's Unabridged Dictionary [MWUD]

The particular noun or noun phrase selected as a term represents merely the tip of the iceberg with respect to meaning. More fundamental is the business *concept* for which the noun or noun phrase stands. This concept *must* be defined. That is, the concept a term represents should never be taken for granted. As one practitioner put it, "The more self-evident the meaning of a term is, the more trouble you can expect." As an example, another practitioner from a medium-sized company rattled off six different (and conflicting!) definitions of "customer" from different parts of his organization.

To communicate business rules effectively, a precise definition for each term should be given explicitly in business-oriented fashion, free of any IT jargon. All wordings (and statements of business rules) that use the term will depend on this meaning. Here is an example of a definition, again from Webster's.

Customer: *one that purchases some commodity or service; especially, one that purchases systematically or frequently*

> Every term requires a careful definition.

The core terms in the business vocabulary — those typically depicted in a graphical fact model — should satisfy these three tests:

Basic: A term should represent something fundamental to business — that is, the term should be one that cannot be derived or computed from any other terms. Any term that can be derived or computed should be specified as the subject of a business rule.

Countable: A term should represent a thing whose instances are discrete — that is, whose instances can be *counted*. A term that has an aggregate or *mass* sense (e.g., *merchandise, personnel, inventory,* and so on) should be broken down into its countable constituents (e.g., *product, employee, item,* etc.). Those are the core concepts of the business vocabulary.

Non-Procedural: A term should always represent a thing we can know something about, rather than how something happens. In other words, a business vocabulary is about *knowledge*, not about the actions, processes, transforms, or procedures that produce or use that knowledge. A business vocabulary, for example, might include the terms *customer* and *order*, but it would not include any action for *taking* customer orders.

The collection of all terms and definitions that satisfy the tests above are the core part of a *business vocabulary*. Such terms are crucial for expressing business rules effectively.

Basing all business rule statements on a shared business vocabulary is the way to avoid a "Tower of Business Babel" when organizing business operations or developing IT requirements for systems to support them. Actually, the same is true for just about any day-to-day work product you could write. Here then is a fundamental (and obvious) principle: We will inevitably work more effectively if we all speak the same language!

> Effective business communication requires a shared business vocabulary.

Developing the Business Vocabulary

Core terms in a business vocabulary represent types or *classes* of things in the business, rather than *instances* of those classes. For example, a business might have 10,000 customers, but they are represented by the single term *customer*. Incidentally, since the term refers to the class rather than to all the instances, the term's singular form is preferred in the business vocabulary (that is, *customer* rather than *customers*).

Business rules generally address classes rather than instances. But business rules can addresses instances too — for example, a business rule might apply to one country, say The Netherlands, that does not apply to another country, say Belgium.

Creating a shared business vocabulary covering both classes and pre-established instances (e.g., The Netherlands, Belgium, etc.) is an important up-front cost of doing business effectively in today's ever more knowledge-intensive world. This activity requires a measure of vision and patience.

The business benefits, however, are substantial. Managing, operating, and interacting based on agreed vocabulary is basic not only to improving business communication, but to retaining core business 'know how' as well. These are hardly luxuries in a world where staffs are ever more volatile, self-service is rapidly becoming the norm, and delivery platforms are forever evolving.

About Connections Between Noun Concepts and Wordings that Represent Them

Noun concepts can be connected to each other much as ligaments connect bones in the human skeleton. Connections between noun concepts are generally expressed using verbs and verb phrases relating appropriate terms. These noun-and-verb constructions are called *wordings* — phrases of predictable types that permit sentences, especially expressing business rules, to be made for business operations.

Examples of wordings are given in the table. Note that each wording involves a verb or verb phrase (italicized in the table) to connect relevant terms. Selection of the best verbs and verb phrases to succinctly represent connections between noun concepts is fundamental to building a robust business vocabulary.

Wording for a Connection Between Noun Concepts	Sample Business Rule Statement Using the Wording
customer *places* order	A customer has always *placed* at least one order.
shipment *is approved by* employee	A shipment must *be approved by* at least two employees.
shipment *includes* order	A shipment must not *include* more than 10 orders.

Here are some important observations:

1. Wordings extend the common business vocabulary in important ways. Most obvious is that wordings add standard verbs and verb phrases. Less obvious but equally important is that by connecting terms they bring structure to the business vocabulary (think ligaments). For this reason, we like to say structured business vocabulary.

2. The sample wordings in the table actually represent types of connections, called *fact types*, rather than individual connections, called *facts*. For example, for *customer places order* an actual fact might be *Global Supply, Inc. has placed the order A601288*. Structured business vocabularies are generally more concerned with identifying fact types rather than actual facts.

3. A fact type is always worded with a verb or verb phrase (wording); therefore fact types are often called *verb concepts*.

> A structured business vocabulary includes
> wordings for verb concepts (fact types).

4. In English and many other languages, every wording follows a strict subject-verb-object structure — for example, *customer places order*. The wording thus provides a building block for constructing sentences of arbitrary complexity that unambiguously express business rules or other kinds of knowledge.

> A wording provides a building block
> for writing unambiguous sentences.

15

5.   A fact type does not imply or establish any business rule on its own, nor does any associated wording. For example, the wording *customer places order* creates no business rule. It would be inappropriate to express a wording as: *A customer has always placed at least one order*. This latter statement is more than a fact type — it expresses a business rule pertaining to the fact type.

> A fact type recognizes something that can be known,
> but implies no business rules on its own.

6.   Verbs (e.g., *places*) used in wordings do not represent or label any action, task, or procedure per se (e.g., *place order*). Any such operation represents a different aspect of business operations — the power or "muscle" aspect. Think of a structured business vocabulary as providing the most appropriate way to organize knowledge about the *results* (or potential results) of such operations. By *most appropriate*, I mean anomaly-free and semantically-clear. In other words, a business vocabulary organizes what we can know as the results of operational processes or transforms taking place in the business.

> A structured business vocabulary organizes knowledge
> about the results of processes or transforms,
> not about how they actually take place.

7.   A majority of connections of core interest for structured business vocabularies involve exactly two terms — e.g., *customer places order*. Connections involving more than two terms, however, are sometimes appropriate (e.g., person *visits* city *on* date). It's also possible for a wording to concern only a single term (e.g., person *smokes*). Refer to Part 2 for discussion.

8.   In formal logic, each wording represents a *predicate*. More precisely, in SBVR a wording represents the *meaning* of a predicate. Although not directly important for practitioners, this point is a crucial one for engineers and others concerned with tooling and formalisms.

Certain important kinds of connections between noun concepts come in handy, *pre-defined* 'shapes'. Chapter 6 discusses four of these, two of which are illustrated briefly below. These special-purpose elements of structure extend the reach and precision of the structured business vocabulary significantly.

Special-Purpose Element of Structure	Example	Use in a Sample Business Rule Statement
Categorization	'Corporate customer' *is a category of* 'customer'.	A customer is always considered corporate if the customer is not an individual person.
Property	order *has* date taken order *has* date promised	An order's date promised must be at least 24 hours after the order's date taken.

A structured business vocabulary establishes the full scope of potential discourse (in business operations and any supporting systems) in a very fundamental way. If a worker or some automated process produces or expresses knowledge about some other concept or connection not in the vocabulary, we literally have no way to communicate or share such knowledge in a standard and consistent fashion.

> A structured business vocabulary establishes the basis for communicating and sharing operational business knowledge.

Using Graphical Fact Models

You might have noticed that even though structured business vocabularies are often rendered graphically, no diagrammatic examples have yet been presented. This is not because diagrams are not useful. Just the opposite is true; they are *very* useful.

Rather, I wanted to emphasize that a structured business vocabulary is first and foremost about what we can *know*, and about how we can *communicate* about what we can know. The bottom line is business communication. Knowledgeable workers on the business side must originate and understand the vocabulary.

> "What we can know" about the operational business can always be expressed on the basis of a structured business vocabulary.

Getting all the terms and wordings in a vocabulary to fit together as if in some large jigsaw puzzle can be hard. This is where a graphical fact model plays an important role.

When creating a blueprint for remodeling your house, you can quickly see when the pieces are not fitting together. The eye often spots the problems quite easily. A graphical fact model serves a similar purpose in developing a business vocabulary. Just remember, sponsors and business people should sign off on vocabulary — the terms, definitions, and wordings — *not* on any diagram per se.

> The principal deliverable of fact modeling is a business vocabulary, not a diagram.

Figure 1–1 presents a simple fact model in graphical form. The various connections in this fact model are listed below it. This list includes several that are unlabeled in the diagram — these connections are based on the special-purpose elements of structure mentioned earlier.

> A fact model is a blueprint for basic business knowledge.

Figure 1–1. Sample Fact Model for a Library.

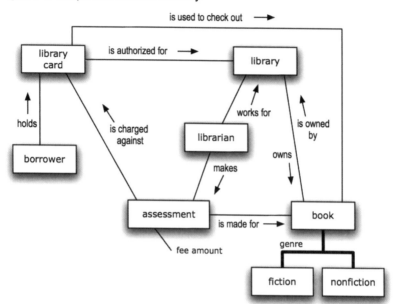

Connections in Figure 1–1

Explicitly-labeled:

- library card is used to check out book
- library card *is authorized for* library
- library *owns* book (book *is owned by* library)
- librarian *works for* library
- librarian *makes* assessment
- assessment *is made for* book
- assessment *is charged against* library card
- borrower *holds* library card

Unlabeled, based on connector type:

- fiction *is category of* book
- nonfiction *is category of* book
- assessment *has* fee amount

Closing the Communications Gap

Ask managers and workers in the business what they mean by *requirements* for developing software systems, and typically you get answers centered on functions to be performed, or on the look-and-feel of user interfaces. The answer "business vocabulary" (or "shared business vocabulary") is almost never among the responses. Nonetheless, a shared, well-structured business vocabulary is indeed a kind of requirement.

> A shared, well-structured structured business vocabulary
> is a kind of requirement.

Like for business rules, a shared, well-structured business vocabulary is by no means the only kind of requirement necessary for software development. Without such a vocabulary, however, you cannot provide real meaning or coherency (sense) to all the others, especially to the business rules. For that reason, a shared, well-structured business vocabulary represents a *fundamental* kind of requirement.

A shared, well-structured business vocabulary literally provides *meaning* (semantics). This meaning, of course, is abstract. It might not be as obvious as what a system does or how the system looks on the outside. Just because something is less obvious, however, does not mean it is any less important. Break a bone, and see what happens to the body's behavior. (I have, so I can speak with some authority!)

> A shared, well-structured business vocabulary provides meaning
> and coherency to other kinds of requirements, especially
> business rules.

The problem is by no means limited to communication of requirements between business workers and IT. Indeed, in many organizations today, business workers from different parts of the organization often have trouble even talking to *each other*. Or to say this more accurately, they talk to each other, but they are not really *communicating*. They live in different *semantic* silos.

A well-managed, well-structured business vocabulary should be a central fixture of business operations. We believe it should be as accessible and as interactive as, say, spellcheck in Microsoft Word.

> A well-managed, well-structured business vocabulary
> should be as accessible and as interactive
> as spellcheck in Microsoft Word.

Special care should be taken for synonyms, as well as for multiple languages. (It's a *global* world these days after all!) See the sidebar.

Note about Synonyms and Multiple Languages

In an ideal world, every operational business concept would have a single name. In real-life, of course, that's not always the case:

- The same noun concept can be given multiple terms. These terms can be in the same language producing *synonyms* (e.g., *customer, client*), in different languages (e.g., French, Mandarin, and so on), or both.
- The same verb concept can be given multiple wordings. These wordings can be in the same language (e.g., customer *places* order, order *is placed by* customer), in different languages (e.g., French, Mandarin, and so on), or both.

A robust environment for managing vocabularies must support this reality. Such support recognizes distinct contexts of usage, as well as communities with different speech preferences.

Developing and managing a shared, well-structured business vocabulary means capturing business knowledge from the business-side workers and managers who possess it (or adopting it from some outside source or community of practice). The skills involved with distilling that business knowledge are essential for business analysts.

You also need appropriate business-level platforms to manage your business vocabulary. Such automated support is crucial to effective business communication, as well as to organizing large sets of business rules. As discussed in Chapter 3, you will need special tooling for this purpose, which we call a *general rulebook system.*

> Your company needs an automated
> business-level work environment for managing
> its operational business vocabulary.

Summary

A good business analyst seeks to ensure that each noun concept and verb concept of the operational business is represented in the business vocabulary, one and only one time. The goal is to ensure that all structural components are *unified* and *unique*. This approach helps ensure that all business rules and other forms of business communication are expressed consistently.

> A structured business vocabulary promotes consistency.

Some IT professionals believe that if they can get behavior right, the structure will simply fall into place. That is not our experience at all. It's the body as a whole that matters. You can design a lot of very elegant appendages and a lot of fancy behaviors, but there had better be a well-considered skeleton to hold them all together!

Chapter 2

What You Need to Know About Business Rules

In the human body, control is provided by the nervous system, an organized collection of nerves that connect to the muscles. Business operations must have similar coordination of behavior. This coordination or *guidance* is supported by business rules.

In the human body, power is provided by the muscles; in business operations, it is supported by processes. Nerves and muscles are separate; business rules and processes should be separate too.

This principle of separation is called *Rule Independence.* Not embedding business rules in processes has huge benefits — not the least of which are for the processes themselves, as discussed in Chapters 11 and 12. The ideas underlying Rule Independence are enumerated in the *Business Rules Manifesto*, a copy of which can be found at the end of this book.

> Rule Independence means separating business rules
> from processes.

Rules are familiar to us all in real life. We play games by rules, we live under a legal system based on rules, we set rules for our children, and so on.

Yet the idea of rules in business systems is ironically foreign to many people. Say "rules" and many IT professionals, for example, think vaguely of expert systems or artificial intelligence — approaches deemed appropriate for only very specialized or very advanced kinds of problems. Recognition has come only slowly about how central business rules actually are to basic, day-to-day business operations.

Not coincidentally, many business-side workers and managers have become so well indoctrinated in *procedural* views for developing requirements that thinking in terms of business rules might initially seem foreign and perhaps abstract. Virtually every methodology has been deficient in this regard, whether for business process reengineering, system development, or software design.

That omission is *highly detrimental and very costly*. Thinking about the control aspect of any organized activity in terms of rules is actually very natural. For example, imagine trying to explain almost any game you can think of — chess, checkers, baseball, football, tennis, and so on — without explaining the rules on which the moves in the game are based. Even if it were possible (that's doubtful!), explaining things that way would certainly not be very *effective*.

> Absence of business rules in IT methodologies is highly detrimental and very costly for the business.

In short, you need business rules. Without any exaggeration, good business rules are no less important to business operations than a robust, finely-tuned nervous system is to the human body.

You naturally want each business rule to be specified *once and only once*. One-place specification (*single-sourcing*) means the business rule will be easier to find — and to change quickly. If you want true agility, business rules are the ticket.

Collectively, the set of business rules represents a separate *rulebook* for the business game. This rulebook should, of course, be automated, to provide scalable support for the origination and management of the business rules. As discussed in Chapter 3, you need special tooling for the rulebook, which we call a *general rulebook system*.

> The rulebook encompasses the rules of the business game.

Do business rules complicate matters for the business? *No!* Doing business is no more complicated by having independent business rules than are the games of chess, baseball, and football by having their own independent rulebooks.

Are business rules all that matter? *Of course not!* You still need artifacts for other needs, including process models, use cases, etc. These latter deliverables are needed to produce the raw power to do work — muscles for the business to flex. Business rules represent a well-developed nervous system, a way to ensure your business works *smart.*

> **Business rules ensure your business works smart.**

The Basics of Business Rules

A first step in understanding business rules is simply to relate them to the issue of guidance. The sidebar below presents a light sampling of typical business rules, each categorized informally according to the kind of guidance it provides. Note how far-ranging these categories really are. *Every* aspect of guidance for business operations can be addressed by business rules.

Restriction
A customer must not place more than three rush orders charged to its credit account.

Guideline
A customer with preferred status should have its orders filled immediately.

Computation
A customer's annual order volume is always computed as total sales closed during the company's fiscal year.

Inference
A customer is always considered preferred if the customer has placed more than five orders over $1,000.

Timing
An order must be assigned to an expeditor if shipped but not invoiced within 72 hours.

Trigger
'Send-advance-notice' must be performed for an order when the order is shipped.

A second step in understanding business rules is to understand how they relate to a structured business vocabulary. Rules build *directly* on fact types. Basically, expression of a business rule simply adds a sense of obligation or necessity to terms and wordings *already* set up in the fact model.

Terms, Facts, and Rules

The focus of business rules has often been described as *terms, facts, and rules.* Under the rigorous formal prescriptions of SBVR this mantra, which dates to the early 1990s work of the Business Rules Group (www.BusinessRulesGroup.org), is not 100% technically accurate. Nonetheless it's memorable and certainly adequate for an initial understanding.

Here is a sample business rule: *A customer must be assigned to an agent if the customer has placed an order.* Figure 2–1 shows the relevant terms and wordings for this statement. Note how the fact types worded *customer places order* and *customer is assigned to agent* are used directly in the statement, with only minor adjustments in tense as appropriate for English grammar.

Figure 2–1. Terms and Wordings for the Agent-Assignment Business Rule.

In business problems involving hundreds or thousands of business rules — not at all uncommon — there is no way to achieve consistency across such large numbers of statements without a common base of terms and wordings. This vocabulary scaffolding is indispensable for *scaling up*.

Scaling up requires that business rules be expressed directly on a structured business vocabulary.

Basing verbalizations directly on wordings for fact types is a key feature of business-oriented notations for business rules such as *RuleSpeak*.

A third step in understanding business rules is appreciating the importance and power of expressing business rules *declaratively*. When statements are based directly on wordings for fact types, the result is always declarative. The Agent-Assignment Business Rule presented above illustrates. Expressing business rules declaratively is a key means of liberating the business from the perils of IT-speak. The sidebar below explains how you can determine whether specifications are declarative.

When Are Specifications Declarative?

In graduate school in the early 1970s, I learned this highly pragmatic test for determining whether specifications are declarative:

- Take each statement of the specification and type it on an individual punch card. (It's really hard to find punch cards these days, but for the sake of discussion, let's ignore that.)

- Assemble the deck.

- Test it to make sure it works.

- Throw the whole deck up in the air.

- Pick up all the cards in random order.

- Re-test it.

If the logic still works, the statements are declarative. If not, they are procedural. The point is that in declarative specifications no logic is lost 'between the lines' — i.e., none is intrinsic to the sequence of presentation. In other words, there is no hidden semantics (meaning).

Fully appreciating these ideas requires careful examination of the relationship between business rules and events. In general, business rules specified declaratively are free of any direct reference to events. More about that important topic in Chapter 8.

Violation of Business Rules

Let's examine more closely business rules that can be violated. Consider the Agent-Assignment Business Rule. What happens when an event occurs that might violate this business rule?

1. The business rule needs to be evaluated with respect to the event. We call that a *flash point*.

2. If a violation is detected, appropriate intervention should ensue.

3. Assuming the user is authorized and knowledgeable, some explanation should be provided about what triggered the intervention. You

might call that explanation an error message, but we prefer *guidance message*. The intent should be to inform and to shape appropriate business behavior, rather than simply reprimand or inhibit it.

What should that guidance message say? *The guidance message should contain exactly the same text as given for the business rule.* For the Agent-Assignment Business Rule it should literally read: *A customer must be assigned to an agent if the customer has placed an order.* To put this more strongly, the business rule statement *is* the guidance message.

> **A business rule statement *is* the guidance message.**

Now I overstated the case a bit to make the point. Obviously, additional or customized text can be provided to explain the relevance of the business rule to the specific event, to suggest corrective measures, to give examples, and so on. Also, in a truly-friendly business rule system, you often wouldn't want simply to present the message, then shut down the work. Instead, as discussed in Part 4, you might offer a procedure or script to the user to assist in taking immediate corrective action. But for now, let's stick to the main point.

And that main point is this: The guidance messages that business workers see once an operational business system is deployed should be the very same business rules that knowledgeable workers on the business side expressed as requirements during development. Guidance messages, business rule statements, rule-related requirements — these are all literally one and the same. Well-expressed business rules during the requirements process mean well-expressed guidance messages; poorly-expressed business rules during the requirements process mean poorly-expressed guidance messages.

This approach has *proven* potential for closing the requirements gap between business people and IT that still plagues many companies today. In traditional approaches, much is usually lost in the translation of up-front requirements into the actual running systems. Using business rules, the business side gets back whatever guidance it puts in — a truly business-oriented approach.

Direct assistance in expressing the business rules up-front will prove very valuable to the managers and workers involved in business rule capture. It will enable them to be far more articulate about their requirements. We see the ability to assist in expressing business rules as a key skill for business analysts. Every business analyst should speak RuleSpeak!

> Business rules help close the requirements gap.

Decisioning

Business rules are not an end in themselves; ultimately, they are about enabling the business to make good, consistent operational *decisions*. (For an excellent book on decisioning, see [Taylor and Raden 2007].) An operational decision is where some minute-to-minute, day-to-day determination must be made in performing business activity. Such a decision typically might have to do with configuration, allocation, assignment, classification, assessment, compliance, diagnosis, and so on.

Generally, operational decisions are concerned with either of the following:

- Coordinating some business process.
- Applying specialized know-how in the context of some product/service.

Examples of operational decisions that fall into the latter category might include whether or not to:

- Approve an application for automobile insurance.
- Pay a claim.
- Buy a stock.
- Declare an emergency.
- Accept a reservation.
- Indicate possible fraud.
- Give an on-the-spot discount to a customer.
- Assign a particular resource to a given request.
- Select a health care service for a patient.
- Certify a ship for safety.

You can expect business rules to generally align according to the kind of operational decision they support — coordinating some business process or applying some specialized know-how.

Examples for three different organizations are given below.

Internal Revenue Service (IRS)

Business Rule for Coordinating a Business Process
- *A processed tax return must indicate the IRS Center that reviewed it.*

Business Rule Applying Specialized Know-How
- *The calculated total income must be computed as tax return wages (line 1) plus tax return taxable-interest (line 2) plus tax return unemployment compensation (line 3).*

Ministry of Health

Business Rules for Coordinating a Business Process
- *A claim must be assigned to an examiner if fraud is suspected.*
- *An on-site audit must be conducted for a service provider at least once every five years.*

Business Rules Applying Specialized Know-How
- *A claim involving comprehensive visits or consultations by the same physician for the same patient must not be paid more than once within 180 days.*
- *A claim that requests payment for a service event that is a provision of health service type 'consultation' may be paid only if the service event results from a referral received from another service provider.*

Ship Inspection Agency

Business Rules for Coordinating a Business Process
- *A ship inspection work order must include at least one attendance date.*
- *A ship must indicate a client who is financially responsible for inspections.*
- *An inspection due for a ship must be considered suspended if the ship is laid-up.*

Business Rules Applying Specialized Know-How
- *A ship area subject to corrosion must be inspected annually.*
- *A salt water ballast tank must be inspected empty if the ship is more than five years old.*
- *A barge must have an approved bilge system to pump from and drain all below-deck machinery spaces.*

Business rules concerning the company's product/service invariably involve the company's special area(s) of expertise. They often use more arcane (knowledge-rich) vocabulary. For that reason, such business rules are typically more difficult to capture and express. And there tends to be significantly more of them. Your methodology needs to be prepared for that.

How far can you take operational decisioning in a company? I don't know the ultimate answer. At the present time, no one does.

But let me try to answer the question a different way. Suppose you take any given operational decision in the business. Is it always possible to capture all relevant business rules such that the decision could be made precisely or optimally with no human intervention? *No*. Some problems are just too difficult — e.g., *accurate* weather forecasting.

In the typical business, however, a large number of crucial everyday decisions come nowhere near that degree of complexity. For all those decisions, you *can* capture all the business rules and make precise or optimal decisions. That's a proven fact.

Summary

Business rules should be externalized from processes and established as a separate resource. Rule Independence permits direct management of the business rules, so they can evolve at their own natural pace rather than that of the software release cycle. Other benefits include better process models, and much closer tie-in to the business side (a.k.a. business alignment). Business rules put your company on the road to *true* agility.

> Business rules put your company on the road to *true* agility.

When introduced to business rules, the first reaction some people have is that their business has far more exceptions to business rules than rules per se. They question how all these exceptions can be handled in any organized fashion. This is a valid concern.

Exceptions to business rules, however, merely represent more business rules. Looking at it that way is crucial — *every business rule costs you something*.

> Every business rule costs something.

 The most significant cost of rules is not the direct cost of their implementation and maintenance in software systems (especially if you're using a rule engine). The real cost often lies hidden in the associated documentation, training, administration, and time — the *people* time it takes to communicate the business rules and to change them. Time, of course, is among the most precious of all commodities. Your business does not need *more* rules — it probably needs fewer (*good*) rules!

Chapter 3

What You Need to Know About Rulebook Management

How many business rules does your company have? A hundred? A thousand? Ten thousand? More? How easy is it to change any one of those rules? How easy is it to determine where the rule is implemented? How easy is it to find out why it was implemented in the first place?

Many companies today are starting to realize they have significant problems in managing their business rules. Often, this perception did not start off that way. Initially, the perception might have fallen under some other label such as *change management*, *data quality*, *knowledge management*, or so on. Call it what you will, these companies are discovering that the business guidance at the core of their day-to-day operations, their essential decision logic, is not being managed in any consistent or coherent manner.

One way or another, every organization will eventually discover the need for managing its business rules. New skills must be acquired and appropriate work environments implemented. Fortunately, pioneering companies have already discovered what these techniques are, and good commercial tools have emerged to support them. These tools and techniques are *already* paying off handsomely.

General Rulebook Systems (GRBS)

We call the kind of automated, specialized, business-level platform your company needs to manage its business rules a *general rulebook system* (GRBS). The purpose of a GRBS is to record, develop, and coordinate business rules, but not 'execute' them per se. Think of a GRBS as more or less the counterpart of a general ledger system, except that the GRBS is for business rules.

> A *general rulebook system* (GRBS) is an automated, specialized, business-level platform for managing business rules.

What should a general rulebook system (GRBS) look like? In one sense, a GRBS is simply a database or repository — one whose interfaces must be business-person-friendly. What should be recorded in it? What additional kinds of support are needed?

Remember that business rules represent business-level decision logic — not programming logic or rules specified for implementation under a rule engine or other software platform. The goal is to give *business* workers and *business* analysts the ability to access and manage decision logic directly. So the focus should be on the kinds of challenges these business workers and analysts face on a day-in and day-out basis.

Repositories supporting IT professionals doing software development or rule authoring under rule engines do not measure up in that regard. Most were engineered primarily for use by IT staff with the goal of designing software applications. The difference is not a trivial one.

Fundamental to supporting *business*-level decision logic is an integrated capability to manage business vocabulary and fact models. When rules number in the thousands — or even 'just' in the hundreds — coordinating terminology is essential. Imagine trying to understand and apply that much decision logic without such coordination. It's hard to emphasize too much the need for business-level coordination of business vocabulary.

Traceability and Corporate Memory

Many questions about business rules (and business vocabulary) that business workers and business analysts will have are quite predictable. Frequently asked questions include those in Table 3–1. Although the importance of these questions is self-evident, most companies have never managed this kind of core knowledge in any coordinated or comprehensive manner.

Table 3–1. FAQs a General Rulebook System (GRBS) Should Support.

- *To which areas of the business does a business rule apply?*
- *What work or decision-making tasks does a business rule guide?*
- *Where is a business rule implemented?*
- *In what jurisdictions is a business rule enforced?*
- *What purpose does a business rule serve?*
- *When was a business rule created?*
- *When did a business rule become effective?*
- *Where and when has the business rule been published?*
- *Are there previous versions of a business rule?*
- *Is a business rule currently in effect?*
- *Has a business rule been retired or replaced, and if so, when and why?*
- *Who is responsible for a business rule?*
- *What influenced the creation or modification of a business rule?*
- *Who can answer particular kinds of questions about a business rule?*
- *Who has been involved with a business rule over time, and in what way?*
- *Has the business rule been adopted by, or from, some outside community of practice?*
- *Where can more information about a business rule be found?*

Another question crucial to rulebook management is being able to address relationships *between* business rules — that is, to easily trace rule-to-rule connections. Business rules can be interconnected in many ways, but the most important are:

- A rule has been interpreted from or into another rule.
- A rule acts as an exception to another rule.
- A rule supports a computation or derivation used by another rule

The first kind of connection above is particularly important. Many business rules are interpretations of what we call *governing* rules — laws, acts, statutes, regulations, contracts, business policies, legal determinations, and so on. Knowing the *who*, *when*, and *why* of such interpretations is crucial in supporting impact assessment when a rule changes. By the way, most business rules do change, sooner or later!

In today's world, discovering or reconstructing the pedigree of a business rule is time-consuming, error-prone, and sometimes impossible. Worse, once discovered or reproduced for a particular need at a point in time, the history is often not retained in any organized fashion for future use. That means the whole process must be repeated the next time it is needed, *ad nauseam*.

To be blunt, our corporate memory about business rules is deeply flawed. And consider this — without memory there can be no *accountability*.

What we have today is actually a risky and very expensive way to do business. The valuable resources consumed could certainly be put to better use. Think of rulebook management as a practical means to create pinpoint corporate memory, always keeping it right at your fingertips.

> Rulebook management is about creating pinpoint corporate memory, always keeping it right at your fingertips.

All the items listed in Table 3–1 illustrate various forms of *traceability*. A GRBS can provide basic support for traceability by means of predefined reports and queries. Beyond that, visualization techniques are quite useful for presenting more complex or highly-interrelated information. Comprehensive support for traceability is a key ingredient in successful rulebook management.

Rulebook Management: the skills, techniques, and processes needed to express, analyze, trace, retain, and manage the decision logic used in day-to-day business operations

Focus: Manage decision logic as a business problem rather than a technical problem.

Goals: Ensure that ...
- Basic business know-how is always accessible to those duly authorized.
- Business policies, regulations, and contractual obligations are interpreted in a faithful, repeatable, and transparent fashion.

Another important aspect of rulebook management is the difficulty of validating large sets of rules, and ensuring that the decision logic is complete, internally consistent, and non-redundant. Automated support in this area is a *must have*. Examples of *rule quality* items:

- A rule is similar to another rule.
- A rule subsumes another rule.
- A rule is logically equivalent to another rule.
- A rule is in conflict with another rule.

Rather than a new chore for the company's thinly stretched resources, such support should be viewed as an important new area of efficiency. Never before has the company's decision logic been in a form that could be checked *before deployment* for true quality by business workers and business analysts from the business point of view.

> Your general rulebook system (GRBS)
> must provide automated quality assessment
> for use by business workers and business analysts.

Smart Governance

Say "governance" and many people immediately think IT governance, or sometimes data governance. *Governance* has been bandied about so much that its meaning has become clouded and trivialized. That's unfortunate, because the true meaning of governance is actually straightforward. And that true meaning has everything to do with meeting today's business challenges.

So bear with me while I do a little refresher on the meaning of "governance". You may be surprised at what pops out! Here's how *governance* is defined in MWUD:

> **Governance** ...
> 1: the act or **process** of governing
> 2a: the office, power, or **function** of governing
> 2b: controlling or directing influence : AUTHORITY
> 3: the state of being governed
> 4a: **the manner or method** of governing : conduct of office
> 4b [obsolete]
> 5: **a system** of governing

So "governance" implies the *process, function, manner or method,* or *system* of governing. It also implies *authority* or the *state of being governed.* Since most of the definitions reference "governing", let's also examine *govern* in MWUD. Note how prominently 'rule' and 'policy' appear in these definitions.

> **Govern** ...
> *transitive verb*
> 1a: to exercise arbitrarily or by established **rules** continuous sovereign authority over; especially: to control and direct the making and administration of **policy** in
> 3a: to control, direct, or strongly influence the actions and conduct of (as a person or a group)
> *intransitive verb*
> 1: to prevail or have decisive influence : CONTROL
> 2: to exercise authority: perform the functions of government especially in the making and execution of **policy**

At the risk of saying the obvious, note that the definitions do not say anything about IT, data, or anything similar. For that matter, they don't even mention processes(!). The definitions do, however, have everything to do with business rules. To demonstrate, take a quick look at the seminal definition of "business rule" from the original GUIDE report in 1995. Note the key words 'control' and 'influence'.

> **Business Rule** [GUIDE, 1995] ... a statement that defines or constrains some aspect of the business ... [which is] intended to assert business structure, or to **control** or **influence** the behavior of the business

The newer definition of 'business rule' in SBVR is based on the following definition of *rule* from the Oxford Dictionary of English. Note the pivotal place of *governing*.

> **Rule**: one of a set of explicit or understood regulations or principles **governing** conduct or procedure within a particular area of activity … a law or principle that operates within a particular sphere of knowledge, describing, or prescribing what is possible or allowable

Here is my point. Business rules and governance are inherently and inextricably linked. The better your company gets at business rules, the better (smarter) it can become at the nuts and bolts of governance. Simple as that. And absolutely as critical as that in a volatile, rapidly changing, and ever more complex (and regulated) world!

What Business Governance Is and How Rulebook Management Relates to It

So what do we mean by *business* governance? A key phrase in the definition of *govern* is: "… the making and administration of policy in." Central to the activity of governing then are:

- How policy and rules are created ("made").
- How policy and rules are deployed (managed, distributed, and monitored) within the actual day-to-day operations of the business ("administration").

Accordingly, our definition for *business governance* is:

> **Business Governance** … a process, organizational function, set of techniques, and systematic approach for creating and deploying policy and business rules into day-to-day business operations

The effectiveness of business governance clearly hinges on the ability to deploy policy and business rules effectively. Such deployment should be *timely, effective, selective, pervasive, traceable, repeatable,* and *retractable.* We also want the activity to be transparent and to be able to hold accountable those parties responsible for specific actions.

For effective deployment, all four aspects mentioned above — a *process, organizational function, set of techniques,* and *systematic approach* — are essential. Given the complexity of the activity, however, the one perhaps most basic is simply having a *systematic approach.*

That's where rulebook management comes to play. As discussed earlier, your company needs a general rulebook system (GRBS). In the context of business governance, a GRBS plays another critical role: *knowledge retention.*

You *will* lose workers. Staff will be downsized or outsourced; your baby boomers will retire; your most critical subject matter expert will win the lottery. If your business rules have not been retained and managed, how do you regain the lost knowledge? One approach is to try to mine business rules from legacy code (not a fun prospect!). The alternative is either reengineering the business systems from scratch or replacing them with expensive (and often painful) deployments of packaged software. Far better — just don't lose the business rules in the first place!

> Never lose your business rules!

So job one in moving toward smarter governance is simply gearing up for a general rulebook system (GRBS). That gives you your systematic approach. Then you can start talking seriously about re-engineering the process of business governance.

Re-Engineering the Governance Process

Yes, Virginia, there is a governance process. Unfortunately, in many companies today the as-is governance process is ad hoc, ragged, and effectively broken. That just won't do, given the complexity, rate of change, and knowledge-intensity of doing business in today's high-tech, globally-connected world. Thinking in the large, how to fix the nuts-and-bolts of the governance process in a highly pragmatic fashion is the most fundamental insight and value-add of the business rules paradigm.

> In many companies today,
> the governance process is effectively broken.

The governance process involves a series of actions and checkpoints (i.e., a workflow) indicating who should be doing what, and when, with respect to deploying policy and business rules. The scope of the governance process includes, but is not limited to:

- Developing internal business policies.
- Evaluating relevant laws, regulations, contracts, agreements, etc.
- Tracing interpretations for both the above.
- Performing reviews.
- Resolving conflicts.
- Coordinating sign-offs.
- Performing impact assessments.
- Coordinating business roll-out (deployment) of new or modified business rules.
- Ensuring the correctness of system-level deployments from the business perspective.
- Assessing when to retract or retire business rules.

A re-engineered governance process should view the workflow from beginning-to-end, encompassing all seven of these tasks:

The Seven Steps of the Governance Process
1. *Assess/review business influences.*
2. *Create/refine business strategy.*
3. *Develop operational business rules.*
4. *Assess/simulate impact.*
5. *Deploy business rules.*
6. *Monitor performance.*
7. *Revise/retire business rules.*

Note the starting points in tasks 1 and 2. These have to do with injecting structured, documented business strategy into the governance process. Can strategy really be structured and effectively documented? Absolutely. Refer to [Lam 1998] and [The Business Motivation Model].

Who should have responsibility for the governance process? Processes need engineering (or more commonly, re-engineering) and for that you need engineers. The governance process specifically needs engineers specializing in governance — *governance engineers*. What goals should they have? All the items in Table 3–2. Ultimately, *this* is what rulebook management is all about.

Table 3–2. Goals for Governance Engineers.

- **Fiduciary Responsibilities Support.** Demonstrate compliance by officers of the organization with their fiduciary responsibilities.
- **Risk Management.** Enable more effective, timely, and focused management of risks by monitoring performance around critical items of business policy and strategy.
- **Liability Management.** Reduce or eliminate legal and financial liabilities due to non-compliance with contractual obligations and statutory responsibilities.
- **Quality Assurance.** Ensure consistency in business behavior, and appropriate interactions with external stakeholders.
- **Regulatory Compliance.** Ensure conformance with external regulation.
- **Agility.** Ensure timely and coordinated deployment of changes in business policy and strategy.
- **Knowledge Retention.** Ensure that specialized know-how, basic business intellectual property (IP), and core competencies are captured and managed explicitly, so that survivability and sustainability are less dependent on individual workers and their tacit knowledge.
- **Accountability.** Ensure clear lines of responsibility for interpretations and deployments of business policy and regulation into day-to-day operations.
- **Transparency.** Ensure that business activity subject to external regulation is conducted in a manner that can be fully audited.

Summary

This Chapter has emphasized the importance of managing both business rules and business vocabulary, and doing so in concert. These tasks are very unlike managing the artifacts of software development and should not be mixed together. The former should be undertaken purely as a business proposition, using a general rulebook system (GRBS).

Business rules and the governance of the enterprise are inherently and inextricably linked. The implication is that the better your company gets at business rules — and rulebook management — the better it can become at the nuts and bolts of governance. The goal — *smart* governance.

> The goal — *smart* governance.

Part 2

Business Vocabularies and Fact Models

Chapter 4

Verb-ish Models for Verbalization

Let me tell you something we have learned from our work on business rules. The world's leading cause of ambiguity in expressing business rules — and other requirements — is *missing verbs*. The following example illustrates.

> Business Rule: *An order must not be shipped if the outstanding balance exceeds credit authorization.*

As a first-cut statement, that's perhaps not bad. The more you read it, however, the more ambiguity you'll see. Clearly, some important ideas are hidden or missing. For example:

- The outstanding balance *of what?* ...order? ...customer? ...account? ...shipment?
- The credit authorization *of what?* ...order? ...customer? ...account? ...shipment?

The hidden or missing ideas are all verb-related. To eliminate the ambiguity, the relevant verb concepts — a.k.a. *fact types* — must be discerned, then the original business rule restated. Suppose the relevant fact types can be worded as follows:

customer <u>places</u> order

customer <u>has</u> credit authorization

customer <u>holds</u> account

account <u>has</u> outstanding balance

Using RuleSpeak the business rule can now be restated as:

> Revised Business Rule: *An order must not be shipped if the outstanding balance <u>of</u> the account <u>held</u> by the customer that <u>placed</u> the order exceeds the credit authorization <u>of</u> the customer.*

Although the resulting statement is a bit wordier, it is far less likely to be misunderstood, misapplied, or mis-implemented. It is now *enterprise-robust*. Two key insights here are:

1. Wordings for fact types are generally expressed using verbs. Note in particular the verb *holds* (or *held*) and the verb *places* (or *placed*). I'll come back to the pesky preposition 'of' later.

2. Wordings for relevant fact types should always appear *explicitly* in expression of business rules. For that matter, wordings should appear explicitly in *any* form of business communication you want to be unambiguous, including IT requirements.

> To reduce ambiguity in written business communication of all types, including business rules, you must use standard verbs.

Given that verbs are so crucial to effective business communication of all kinds, you might question why data models and class diagrams haven't focused more directly on them. The answer, quite simply, is that these tools weren't created for that purpose. They are first and foremost *design* tools for IT professionals.

What do IT professionals design? In general, they are focused on implementing data containers (e.g., tables) or software objects. That focus leaves them noun-ish, but not also verb-ish. The price we are paying for that shortfall in poor business communication practices is huge.

How can the problem be fixed? The answer is simply that verb-ish things should be included alongside noun-ish things as a fundamental part of any structural modeling. This Chapter explains how.

What It Means to be Verb-ish

Many IT professionals associate verbs only with processes, as in "take order" or "pay invoice" or "hire employee". Nothing in the real-world meaning of 'verb', however, limits its use solely to that concern. Have a look at the MWUD definitions of 'verb' and 'predicate' in the box below. Restricting use of verbs only to the naming of processes, tasks, or actions is very unnatural.

> **Verb:** *a word belonging to that part of speech that characteristically is the grammatical center of a <u>predicate</u> and expresses an act, occurrence, or mode of being ...*
>
> **Predicate:** *[2] the part of a <u>sentence</u> or clause that expresses what is said of the subject and that usually consists of a verb with or without objects, complements, or adverbial modifiers*

Experts in the field of linguistics explain that verbs play a far more crucial role. For example, Steven Pinker says, "A verb, then, is not just a word that refers to an action or state but the chassis of a <u>sentence</u>. It is a framework with receptacles for the other parts ... to be bolted onto" [Pinker 2007, p. 31, emphasis added]. Without verbs, literally there are no sentences.

Sentences are how you communicate effectively. Sentences are what you're reading *right now*. A well-written business rule is always a sentence. In general, all business communication and many forms of business requirements should be sentences. When you start looking at things that way, it becomes obvious that verbs must be an integral part of *any* structural model.

> A well-written business rule is always
> a sentence based on standard verbs.

Let's take a closer look. Without going too deep into philosophical questions, every verb generally has two sides. Yes, you can think of a verb as designating some action. But you can also think of a verb as designating something you can *know*. Take, for example, the verb 'to place', as in a customer *placing* an order. You can look at 'to place' from two perspectives, both valid:

- There is something a customer can <u>do</u> — i.e., *place* an order. That's an <u>action</u> or <u>process</u>.
- There is something that can be <u>known</u> — i.e., that a customer *can place* an order. That's a <u>fact</u>.

The first perspective, of course, is very important. No one is saying you shouldn't model processes. But taking even a cursory look at other challenges facing businesses today suggests the second perspective is also crucial:

- Achieving reusability or sharing of data (data design).
- Providing high-quality information (business intelligence — BI).
- Expressing business rules (criteria for operational decisions).
- Eliminating stove-pipe products (product re-engineering).
- Retaining know-how (knowledge retention).

Verbs are therefore the point of departure for addressing a host of broader needs facing businesses today. Modeling the underlying verb concepts (as well as the nouns they involve) is the purpose of *fact models*. Think of a fact model as a *verbal* model, one serving for more effective *verbalization* of operational business knowledge. It's high time we focus on the basics of business communication as the starting point for everything we do or design.

> A fact model is a *verbal* model, one serving for more effective *verbalization* of operational business knowledge.

Fortunately, fact modeling as a discipline has a long and solid pedigree. It's not something new; it's been around for decades. The gurus of this space include Terry Halpin [Halpin 2008] and Sjir Nijssen [Nijssen 1981]; the standard for the space is SBVR. Actually, this discussion features only two new things:

1. *RuleSpeak* and the now in-depth understanding of how business rules should be based on facts and fact models.

2. The conventions used to represent fact models graphically. We developed this graphical notation in large-scale client projects starting in the mid-1990s to provide a more business-friendly face for fact models.

Issues That Can Only Be Handled Well Using Verbs

Traditional data models and class diagrams fall short in a number of respects in their handling of verbs. The following discussion outlines three of these shortcomings, each addressed effectively in fact modeling. First, two quick points about terminology in the box below.

> **Verb:** For convenience, I say *verb* although I really mean *verb or verb phrase*. For example, 'owns' counts as a verb, but in my usage so too do 'rides in' and 'is being actively marketed'.
>
> **Verb Concept:** SBVR has defined *verb concept* and *fact type* as synonyms. These two terms can be used interchangeably. A verb concept or fact type is always understood to include some relevant noun concept(s) as well as something verb-ish. So the verb 'owns' might be included in the expression of the verb concept (or fact type) 'person *owns* vehicle'.

Unary Fact Types — Verbs about Only One Thing

A unary fact type always provides a simple yes-or-no answer to some basic operational business question. In other words, a unary fact type is always Boolean (i.e., true or false). The following example illustrates.

Figure 4–1. Fact model showing unary fact type.

> **Note on Notation**
> The starburst symbol always indicates 'fact type'. Here, the starburst introduces the verb (phrase) 'is being actively marketed'. The line between the noun concept 'product' and the starburst means nothing on its own; it simply shows where the verb (phrase) fits into the diagram.

The fact type worded 'product is being actively marketed' is unary because it pertains to only one noun concept, product. This unary fact type indicates that a given product either is or is not being actively marketed. The *actual* answer to the question, of course, depends on which particular product is being talked about.

Like any fact type, this unary fact type could be relevant to many kinds of business communications, including statements of business rules. The following sample business rule illustrates.

Business Rule: *A briefing may be given only for a product that is being actively marketed.*

Roles — Noun Concepts Whose Meaning Is All Tied Up with Verbs

Business people often have a special term for a noun concept they use only in the context of some particular fact type. The following example illustrates.

Figure 4–2. Fact model showing a role.

The fact type diagrammed above is: *flight arrives at [destination] city*. The term in brackets, 'destination', is simply a more specific term used to refer to a city when it is a city where a flight arrives. Such a *role* name designates the part (or 'role') the concept 'city' plays in the context of the fact type. It means nothing more than that.

Note on Notation

Like for unary fact types, a line representing a binary fact type means nothing more than the verb used in its wording. The little directional arrow that appears alongside the line simply indicates how to "read" the fact type. The proper wording for the fact type above is therefore understood to be 'plane arrives at [destination] city' — not 'city [destination] arrives at flight' (obviously nonsensical). A starburst is usually omitted for a binary fact type since what the line represents is generally obvious from the context of the diagram.

Roles are not the usual kind of noun-ish things IT professionals generally expect; that is, they are not 'normal' entity types or classes as understood in data models or class diagrams. Rather, the meaning of these noun concepts is inextricably tied to some verb (e.g., 'arrives at').

Role names are a particularly good way to handle terms that directly reflect the particular choice of verb in the wording of a fact type. For example, in the following diagram, the role name 'owner' directly reflects the verb of choice, *owns*.

Figure 4–3. Fact model showing a verb-reflecting role name.

Like any other term, a role name is frequently relevant to many kinds of business communication, including statements of business rules. The following sample business rule illustrates.

Business Rule: *A parking citation may be given only to the <u>owner</u> of a vehicle.*

Reversal — Verbs of the Opposite Persuasion

Even if a data model or class diagram gives a verb in one direction of a relationship, it seldom gives it in the opposite direction. Or if it does, it merely offers a preposition. For example, in the following data model, the opposite direction of the verb 'is involved with' is labeled simply 'of'.

Figure 4–4. Data model showing a preposition for the opposite direction of a fact type.

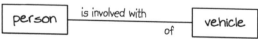

Proper wording for the opposite direction of a fact type, however, is often needed to express business rules or to compose other kinds of business communication or requirement. The following sample business rule illustrates.

Business Rule: *A vehicle must not <u>transport</u> more than 4 passengers.*

In this business rule, the verb 'transport' is used to clearly express the appropriate meaning. Try substituting 'of' in some way into the statement and see how well that works to express the meaning. (It doesn't.) In fact modeling, stand-alone prepositions for fact types are considered lazyman's verbs. Literally, you can't make complete sentences with only prepositions!

> In fact modeling, stand-alone prepositions for fact types are considered lazyman's verbs.

Actually, the communication problem gets even worse. In the real world, people can be involved with vehicles in different ways. 'Passenger' in the business rule above suggests just one way. Suppose that people and vehicles can 'be involved' with each other in at least four ways:

- People own vehicles.
- People lease vehicles.
- People drive vehicles.
- People ride in vehicles.

In data models, such differential 'involvements' are typically handled using a type code treated as 'intersection data'. The following data model illustrates.

Figure 4–5. Data model showing a type code treated as intersection data.

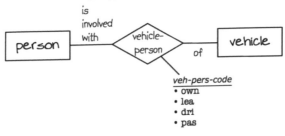

This data model features a new noun-ish thing 'vehicle-person', in which the type code 'veh-pers-code' has been included. Four values of the type code are listed to distinguish the four kinds of 'involvements' from above.

Let's see what now happens to the expression of the passenger business rule. We started with this:

Business Rule: *A vehicle must not <u>transport</u> more than 4 passengers.*

Using the terminology provided by the data model, the rule might now be expressed like this:

Rule: *A vehicle must not be <u>of</u> more than 4 people*
where veh-pers-code = "pas".

Do we really want business communications to sound like that?! *No!* The statement contorts the meaning (mangles the semantics) almost beyond recognition. Besides losing the clarity of 'transports', we've forced the business people to speak in terms of a type code. That's unnatural. This example clearly illustrates the difference between a true *business* rule (the original version) versus what must be considered a *data* rule or *system* rule (the mangled version).

To emphasize this latter point, let's consider a bit more complicated business rule pertaining to *two* kinds of 'involvements'. First, here is the rule verbalized as a business person might expect:

Business Rule: *A person must not <u>lease</u> a vehicle the person <u>owns</u>.*

Using the vocabulary of the data model above, however, we get the following verbalization:

Rule: *A person must not be involved with the same vehicle where veh-per-code = "lea" and veh-per-code = "own".*

Clearly, the more complicated the business rule, the worse the mangling. And a great many of your business rules are *very* complicated! Without further ado, let's simply agree that's awful and move on. The following diagram indicates how these semantics (verb concepts) would be fully handled in fact modeling.

Figure 4–6. Fact model showing multiple 'involvements'.

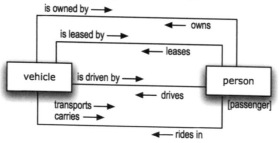

Some key observations:

1. Fact types are always bi-directional (or multi-directional) even if not worded as such explicitly. (All the fact types above have been worded in both directions for the sake of completeness.) Fact models then are very different from process models, which always designate uni-directional flows.

2. Two or more noun-ish things can be related more than once if the meanings of the verbs are different. This differentiation has resulted in the four fact types above.

3. Any verb concept can have a synonym if the meaning is considered *exactly* the same by the business. In the diagram above, for example, the verbs 'transports' and 'carries' are indicated to be synonyms in the context of the given fact type.

Now back to the business rules. The fact model gives us all the scaffolding we need to verbalize the business rules succinctly and naturally. You can verify that for yourself:

Business Rule: *A vehicle must not <u>transport</u> more than 4 <u>passengers</u>.*

Business Rule: *A person must not <u>lease</u> a vehicle the person <u>owns</u>.*

Using the fact model as a blueprint, we can have a real business conversation with business people and subject matter experts *in natural language* about whether these business rules are valid and complete. Indeed, business analysts should ask some hard questions, including perhaps the following.

- Is the person who *drives* a vehicle considered a passenger?
- Does the business rule also apply to *buses*, or just to passenger cars?
- Does the business rule mean a vehicle can't carry more than 4 passengers *ever*, or just at any given point in time?
- Can the *same* person be a passenger in the *same* vehicle more than one time over time?
- *Why* do we really care how many passengers ride in a vehicle?

The answers to these questions could well indicate that the current fact model is incomplete. For example, if the business rules are from a city government, we might actually want to talk about when to issue *traffic citations*. The actual business rules might be:

> Business Rule: *A passenger overload <u>traffic citation</u> must be written for a passenger vehicle carrying more than 4 passengers.*

> Business Rule: *A <u>traffic citation</u> may be given only to a person driving.*

The noun concept *traffic citation* (and related fact types) does not appear in the fact model above. Clearly, some work on that is in store. Now ask yourself this: Would you rather work this out *before* or *after* you get to a data model or class diagram? The answer, I think, speaks for itself.

My point is this. The fundamental problem in business today is not design or implementation of databases or systems. Rather, it is the challenge of business communication. If you can't clearly communicate (verbalize) what you know, you'll never get the database or system you want.

> If you can't clearly communicate (verbalize) what you know, you'll never get the database or system you want.

Where does that take you? Directly to writing complete sentences, which in turn brings you straight to verbs. There's simply nowhere else to turn.

More Ways in Which Fact Models are Verb-ish

Fact models are verb-ish in even more ways than discussed thus far. Two additional areas are examined next.

Objectification

In natural language, we often turn verbs into nouns or noun phrases so we can talk about them as *things*. Doing that is called nominalization; often the intent is to objectify the verbs. (The MWUD definition of *objectify* is: [1a] *to cause to become or to assume the character of an object*.) For example, we might objectify the fact type worded 'person [owner] owns vehicle' into the noun-ish thing *ownership*. The following diagram illustrates, using a dotted line to show that the fact type has been objectified.

Figure 4–7. Fact model showing objectification.

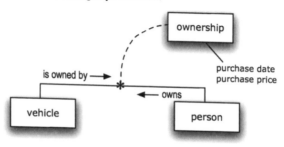

Because objectifications (e.g., 'ownership') are things, they can have properties. For example, *ownership* might have the following two properties, as illustrated in the diagram.

- *Purchase date* — the date a given vehicle was purchased by a given person.

- *Purchase price* — the price paid for a given vehicle by a given person.

All these terms, including the one given to the objectification, are likely to be relevant to business rules. The following sample business rule illustrates.

Business Rule: *Proof of purchase must be provided to establish* <u>*ownership*</u> *of a vehicle.*

States

How do we talk about some potential *state* of something in everyday language? We naturally use a *past participle*, another verb-ish construct. The following diagram illustrates informally for the noun concept *order*.

Figure 4–8. Informal representation of states for 'order'.

In this example, six states have been identified for the normal life cycle ('happy life') of *order*. Each has been identified using a past participle: *received, credit-checked, filled, shipped, invoiced,* and *completed*. A quick look at the MWUD definitions of 'past participle' and 'participle' puts this usage into perspective. Note especially the words *completed action* — that sense is an important one for business rules, as we'll see momentarily.

> **Past Participle:** *a participle that typically expresses* <u>*completed*</u> <u>*action*</u> ...
>
> **Participle:** *[1]: a word having the characteristics of both verb and adjective; especially: the English verbal adjective ending in -ing or in -ed, -d, -t, -en, or -n*

One especially important use of unary fact types in fact modeling is to represent states of noun-ish concepts, as the following formalization of the above diagram illustrates.

Figure 4–9. Fact model for the 'happy' states of 'order' using unary fact types.

Six unary fact types are represented in this diagram. Each unary fact type is given a wording that involves a past participle representing a particular state (completed action) in the life cycle of 'order'. Shown below each unary fact is a role name for an order in that particular state:

- A *received order* is an order for which 'order is received' is true.

- A *credit-checked order* is an order for which 'order [received order] is credit-checked' is true.

- A *filled order* is an order for which 'order [credit-checked order] is filled' is true.

- … and so forth.

Note on Notation

The particular manner in which the unary fact types have been specified requires the states be strictly cumulative:

- *Credit-checked order* requires that the order 'is [already] received'.

- *Filled order* requires that the order 'is [already] received' *and* 'is [already] credit-checked'.

- *Shipped order* requires that an order 'is [already] received' *and* 'is [already] credit-checked' *and* 'is [already] filled'.

- … and so forth.

Organizing the states to be cumulative like this is not required, but seems useful for the example.

The resulting state-oriented vocabulary for 'order' is a rich (and simple) one for verbalizing business rules — for example:

Business Rule: *A <u>credit-checked</u> order must be verified by at least 3 references.*

Business Rule: *A <u>shipped</u> order must be assigned to a carrier.*

Business Rule: *An expeditor must be assigned to an order <u>shipped</u> but not <u>invoiced</u> for more than a week.*

For an order to attain any given state, it must satisfy all business rules pertaining to that state. To say that differently, think of a state as reflecting a *completed action*. For the action to have been completed successfully, it must have satisfied all relevant business rules. Otherwise, it should fail. The following example illustrates.

Figure 4–10. Fact model showing an 'unhappy' state of 'order'.

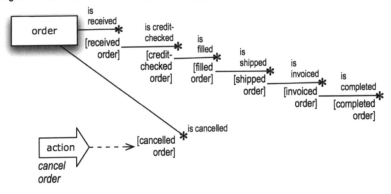

A new unary fact type worded 'order [cancelled order] is cancelled' appears in this diagram. This new fact type can be used to indicate that an order has been cancelled.

Best Practice

A best practice is modeling states is to avoid including 'unhappy' states such as this one within the 'happy life'. Such segregation yields the best results for expressing business rules.

Presumably, canceling an order requires some action (or task or process). To illustrate, an action 'cancel order' has been added informally to the diagram. (Actions are not shown in proper fact models.)

The result the action seeks (a cancelled order) can come about only if business rules allow, for example:

Business Rule: *A <u>cancelled</u> order must not have been <u>shipped</u>.*

Under this business rule, the action can achieve the desired state *cancelled order* only if the order has not already been shipped. The state *shipped order* is therefore a *prohibited antecedent.*

A state reflects a completed action. For an action to complete successfully, it must satisfy all relevant business rules.

Note that the business rule is not embedded in the action, but rather has been specified separately. Specification of business rules apart from processes is the essence of Rule Independence.

Coming full circle to points made earlier, every verb can be seen from two perspectives — as representing action (processes) or as representing knowledge. Invoking *cancel order*, a process, results in a cancelled order, a fact or bit of knowledge. Business rules fall naturally on the knowledge side. Once you liberate verbs from an exclusive process role, liberating the business rules is the next logical step. And what a powerful thing to do!

Summary

Data models and class diagrams are generally created to serve design purposes. If they include verbs at all, they are not vetted against business rules or other forms of operational business communication.

A fact model, in contrast, provides the basis for consistent and unambiguous *verbalization* of business rules and other forms of operational knowledge. Verbalization depends on well-constructed sentences, which in turn puts a premium on verbs. As a result, fact models not only address the problem of designing IT artifacts, but the broader problem of business communication.

> A fact model not only addresses the problem of designing IT artifacts, but the broader problem of business communication.

It is time to recognize full-fledged human communication as the starting point for anything textual (verbal) we write about business operations, including business rules and IT requirements. Fact models provide the necessary scaffolding.

Chapter 5

Creating a Fact Model

How do you create a fact model? You start by identifying the basic terms of the operational business and defining the noun concepts they designate. You build on that by identifying basic verb-ish concepts. What does *basic* mean? *Basic* means that a concept cannot be derived or computed from any other, a least not within scope.

You organize the emerging vocabulary as a graphical fact model. Just in case I need to say this: There should be only a single fact model for the entire scope of your effort. The goal is to create a *shared* vocabulary.

In fact modeling, everything eventually comes around to developing good definitions, so let's focus on that first.

Forming Definitions

A first principle in defining terms is that any aspect of operational business knowledge that might change over time should be treated as a business rule. In forming definitions, therefore, the practitioner should always focus on what is unlikely to ever change — that is, on the fundamental *essence*. (This focus is one of our best practices in Proteus. It is supported, but not necessitated, by SBVR.)

> In defining basic concepts, focus on essence.

For example, consider the following definition of *customer* proposed by a practitioner in a real-life project.

Customer: *an organization or individual person that has placed at least one paid order during the previous two years*

Areas of business practice that could change over time are:

- That a customer is *always* an organization or an individual person.
- That *placing orders* is the core criterion for being a customer.
- That a minimum of exactly *one* order is a criterion for being a customer.
- That an order having been *paid* is a criterion for being a customer.
- That the timeframe of exactly *two* years is a criterion for being a customer.

Now consider the MWUD definition of *customer* (2a):

Customer: *one that purchases some commodity or service; especially one that purchases systematically or frequently*

In contrast to the earlier definition, the MWUD version is clearly an *essence definition* and is therefore much better. The embedded business practices of the practitioner's definition should be treated as business rules:

Business Rule: *A customer must be an organization or individual person.*

Business Rule: *A customer has always placed at least one paid order during the previous two years.*

> A business practice subject to change should be treated as a business rule, not embedded in a definition.

You might have noticed the lack of periods at the end of the definitions given above. This omission is intentional, reflecting standard dictionary practice. (Check MWUD to confirm that for yourself!) A definition is not a sentence (unless you deliberately make it into one by saying: *An x is a y that...*). See the sidebar below to find out why.

Why No Period at the End of a Definition

A definition should be viewed as a phrase or expression that can be substituted for the corresponding term in any sentence (e.g., any business rule statement) where the term appears, without any change in the meaning of the sentence. Of course, such substitution would often produce very long sentences, but the notion does serve to ensure the fitness (or literally the 'fit') of each definition.

Capturing Fact Types and Roles

At its core, a fact model is about fundamental connections between noun concepts, stripped of quantification and qualification. Consider the business rule from above: *A customer has always placed at least one paid order during the previous two years.* The fundamental connection between the two central noun concepts, 'customer' and 'order', is *places*. The appropriate wording for this fact type is *customer places order*. That really gets down to *barebones* knowledge!

> A fact model represents barebones knowledge.

In arriving at the fact type worded *customer places order*, we stripped away the following:

Quantification: *at least one*

Qualification: *paid*; *during the previous two years*

We also stripped away the articles 'a' and 'the' in the sentence. A wording just gives you the right verb or verb phrase to use for a fact type; it's a building block for sentences, but never a sentence per se.

> A wording for a fact type is a building block for sentences.

Graphically, the fact type can be represented as in Figure 5–1.

Figure 5–1. Graphical representation of a fact type.

A key question in fact modeling is whether two wordings mean the same thing or something different (i.e., represent the same fact type or not). Usually, but not always, the answer is obvious. For example, *order is placed by customer* is obviously just a different wording for the fact type meant by *customer places order*. These two wordings express only one underlying fact type. Literally, they are two ways to call out the same meaning.

Should the second wording be included in the fact model? In practice, the answer has to do with scaling up. In the early stages of developing a fact model, additional wordings are not usually necessary. Later on, as the number of business rules grows, additional wordings are unavoidable. For example, consider this new business rule: *A rush order that is placed by a high-risk customer must be paid in advance.* Figure 5–2 illustrates how this second wording should now be included.

Figure 5–2. A fact type with two wordings.

Sometimes, it is not as obvious as in the example that two wordings share the same meaning. Consider *household includes person* and *person belongs to household.* Same meaning? Maybe, although unlike *places* and *is placed by* in the previous example, *includes* and *belongs to* are not merely different forms of the same verb. A practical test would be to ask: Does *person is included in household* always involve exactly the same real-world facts as *person belongs to household*?

Probably so. The same is also probably true for *household includes person.* So these three wordings probably express a single fact type.

Assuming that a single fact type is represented, the wordings should be shown as in Figure 5–3.

Figure 5–3. A fact type with two wordings that use different verbs.

> If two or more wordings share the same meaning,
> they represent just one fact type.

Business people often have a special term for a noun concept they use only in the context of some particular fact type. For example, in the fact type just discussed, business people are likely to say *household includes household member* and *household member belongs to household.* Upon inspection we find that *household member* is simply a more specific term used to refer to a *person* belonging to a household. In other words, the term is a *role.* It can be shown graphically as in Figure 5-4.

Figure 5–4. A role in the context of a fact type.

> A role indicates the part a noun concept
> plays in the context of a fact type.

Note that 'household member' is *not* a synonym of 'person'. To be a synonym, a term must mean *exactly* the same thing as another term. The practical test for *exactly the same thing* is whether each term could be substituted for the other term in *every* sentence (e.g., a business rule statement) where either term appears. That's certainly not the case for *household member* and *person*.

Creating a Fact Model: Case Study

A simple case study illustrates how development of a fact model typically proceeds. Consider a community college that has multiple campuses offering various courses. A first fact type for their fact model might be worded *campus offers [course taught] course,* as illustrated in Figure 5-5.

Figure 5–5. A first fact type for the community college fact model.

Both campus and course would probably have properties (e.g., *address* and *date opened* for campus, and *course name* for course), but let's ignore those details and stick to developing core concepts. (More about properties in the next Chapter.) A second fact type for the community college might be worded *student enrolls in campus,* as indicated in Figure 5–6.

Figure 5–6. Adding a second fact type to the community college fact model.

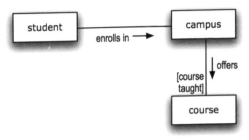

Note that no dependencies are assumed to exist between the two fact types; in other words, any specific case of each can stand on its own. By *stand on its own* I mean:

- Any specific case of *campus offers [course taught] course* can exist:
  - *independently* of whether any student enrolls in that campus.
  - *before* any student enrolls in that campus.

- Any specific case of *student enrolls in campus* can exist:
  - *independently* of whether any course is offered by that campus.
  - *before* any course is offered by that campus.

The community college would probably want business rules to restrict some of those possibilities. If so, the business rules must be explicit — the fact model doesn't assume them. For example, suppose the community college has a business practice not to enroll students in a campus that does not (yet) offer any courses. (Sounds reasonable!) Such a business practice should be expressed as: *A student may enroll in a campus only if the campus offers some course.*

A fact model never assumes any business rule.

To continue with the case study, if courses are being offered by a campus, and students are enrolled, the students will naturally want to sign up for courses. For that we need a third fact type, which can be worded *student signs up for course.* This new fact type in included in Figure 5–7.

Figure 5-7. Adding a third fact type to the community college fact model.

```
  student ─────────── campus
         enrolls in ──▶

    │ signs          │ offers
    ▼ up for  [course ▼
              taught]
                     course
```

Does the community college permit a student to sign up for a course if the course is not offered at a campus in which the student is enrolled? *Probably not.* Assuming the answer is *no*, the following business rule should be specified: *A student may sign up for a course only if the student is enrolled in a campus that offers the course.*

To continue, the community college would probably want to know some things about a student enrolling at a campus — for example, *when* a given student enrolled in a given campus. How would the property *date enrolled* be handled in the fact model?

Date enrolled is not about either a student on his/her own or a campus on its own. Rather, *date enrolled* is about the connection between *student* and *campus* — that is, *date enrolled* pertains to the fact type worded *student enrolls in campus*. In fact

modeling, however, only noun concepts can have properties, not fact types. A fact type (think *verb* concept) is just the meaning of some verb involving noun concepts. It doesn't make sense for a verb concept to have a property. What do we do?

> Fact types cannot have properties — only noun concepts can.

To handle *date enrolled* we need to objectify the fact type — that is, turn the fact type worded *student enrolls in campus* into a noun concept, say *enrollment*. Because enrollment does represent a noun concept, it *can* have a property. Figure 5–8 shows *enrollment* as an objectification of the fact type using a dashed line. *Date enrolled*, in turn, is indicated as a property of *enrollment.*

Figure 5–8. Objectifying a fact type in the community college fact model.

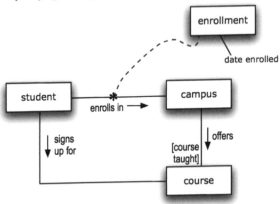

Here's a quick summary of results from our work on the community college. The fact model currently includes:

- Four basic noun concepts, each about a different kind of thing — represented by the terms *student, campus, course,* and *enrollment.*
- Two additional noun concepts — represented by the terms *course taught* (the name of a role) and *date enrolled* (the name of a property).
- Four fact types worded as follows:
  - *campus offers [course taught] course*
  - *student enrolls in campus*
  - *student signs up for course*
  - *enrollment has date enrolled*
- One objectification — the fact type worded *student enrolls in campus* has been objectified as *enrollment.*

Note to the Practitioner

Something this case study does not illustrate very well is the size of a typical fact model, which can easily grow into the dozens or hundreds of terms. To *scale up*, you need an automated tool. Ideal support for graphical representation includes:

- Faithful coordination with all textual data about the vocabulary.
- Intelligent display across multiple pages or tabs. We call these pages or tabs *neighborhoods.*

Unary, Binary, and N-ary Fact Types

Since each of the four fact types in the case study involves exactly two noun concepts, each is a *binary* fact type. The central fact types of a fact model are typically binary. Other fact types, however, can be *unary* (that is, involve only one noun concept) or *n-ary* (that is, involve more than two noun concepts).

To illustrate, suppose a company builds and markets complex products. Owing to the products' costs and complexity, the company focuses on products being actively marketed. Also, the company's sales representatives often receive special briefings about some specific product by some experienced engineer. At least the following two kinds of knowledge (facts) are therefore required:

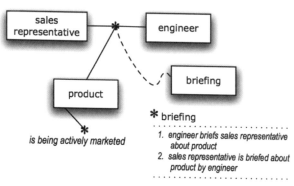

- To know whether a product is being actively marketed.

- To know which engineer briefs which sales representative about which product.

Note that the former item refers to only a single noun concept, *product*. The fact type worded *product is being actively marketed* is therefore *unary*. The second item refers to three: *product, engineer,* and *sales representative*. The fact type worded *engineer briefs sales representative about product* is therefore *n-ary*. Figure 5–9 illustrates how these two fact types can be represented in a fact model.

Figure 5–9. Representing unary and n-ary fact types.

briefing
1. *engineer briefs sales representative about product*
2. *sales representative is briefed about product by engineer*

69

- A unary fact type always provides a simple *yes-or-no* answer to some question (i.e., is Boolean). The unary fact type worded *product is being actively marketed* provides answers to the question, "Is a given product being actively marketed?" Such state-related knowledge is often relevant to business rules — for example: *A briefing may be only for a product that is being actively marketed.*

- The n-ary fact type worded *engineer briefs sales representative about product* cannot be worded in a practical, unambiguous manner using the three connection lines intersecting at the asterisk. Try it. Note that a second wording is *sales representative is briefed about product by engineer.* That one — and any others — must be worked in too. So these wordings are simply annotated separately.

Elementary Fact Types

Every fact type in a fact model should be *elementary*. For each fact type that includes two or more noun concepts, *elementary* means it should not be possible to break the fact type down into two or more other fact types, each with fewer noun concepts, without losing knowledge.

For example, suppose a briefing were set up to accomplish one or more of the following:

- Cover multiple products.
- Update multiple sales representatives.
- Involve multiple engineers.

In that case, a briefing is not always selective to a particular *combination* of engineer, sales representative, and product. Replacing the n-ary fact type by two or three individual fact types (as appropriate), each involving only two noun concepts, would not lose any selective knowledge (facts). By the way, elementary fact types involving three noun concepts, and especially ones with four or more, are *rare* for basic business operations and know-how.

> A fact model should include only elementary fact types.

A good fact model is a relatively *stable* one with respect to potential changes in business practice. Suppose, for example, that the fact type worded *engineer briefs sales representative about product* does accurately reflect current business practice. Will that always be the case? Is there any reasonable chance that in the future the business night want to set up a briefing that covers multiple products, updates multiple sales representatives, or involves multiple engineers? The objectification can't handle any of those things. The business might also want to have the same sales representative briefed about the same product by the same engineer more than one time, over time (and know about it). The objectification can't handle that either. An objectification is simply a verb concept directly transformed into a noun concept — never anything more. Remember: No hidden semantics!

The safest approach (i.e., the approach most accommodating of future changes) is therefore the following:

- Indicate *briefing* to be a noun concept in its own right, not simply an objectification.

- Include in the fact model three binary fact types worded: *briefing is given to sales representative*; *briefing is given by engineer*; and *briefing covers product.*

- Specify one or more business rules if current business practice limits each briefing to just one sales representative, to just one engineer, or to just one product.

In other words, the best approach is to *generalize* the fact model as much as is reasonable, letting business rules handle current and future business practices. The key word in that is *reasonable*. What does *reasonable* mean? *Reasonable* means that there is a chance the business practice will change. If the business practice will assuredly never change, then generalizing the fact model for that possibility is *not* reasonable.

> Generalize the fact model as much as is reasonable;
> handle more restrictive business practices — current
> or future — using business rules.

Summary

In the past, many business people and subject matter experts have been intimidated by data models, class diagrams, and similar IT-centric artifacts. That's unfortunate. A fact model should never be viewed as representing anything more than just what it is — a structured business vocabulary covering the basic concepts of business operations.

It does take some practice and patience to learn the ropes. After all, a fact model is based on conventions that require discipline.

Beyond that though, understanding a fact model isn't really that hard — *if* you understand the basic knowledge implicit in business operations. The fact model simply makes that basic knowledge explicit. So if a fact model does prove harder to understand than understanding the basic knowledge of business operations, somebody is simply doing something wrong.

Chapter 6

Special-Purpose Elements of Structure

The focus of Chapter 5 was primarily on verb concepts (fact types) whose shape (business meaning) lies completely with the wordings supplied for them by business workers and business analysts. Such verb concepts have no implicit or prefabricated meaning of any kind.

Other important elements of structure come in handy, *pre-defined* shapes. This chapter illustrates use of four of these shapes, as presented in Table 6–1. These special-purpose connections between noun concepts provided by SBVR extend the reach and precision of the fact model significantly. Before I get too deeply into that, however, I should give a quick note about the term *instance*.

About the Term *Instance*

At this point in the discussion, I will start taking a few liberties with the SBVR concept of *instance*. In SBVR, instances are always in the real world, not in a model. For example, you can't put the real country Canada into a model. Wouldn't exactly fit(!). In a fact model, you can include only concepts (like the one that stands for Canada) and facts (things you assert are true about Canada).

If you're used to thinking about instances being organized within or by a model (e.g., to be stored in a database), however, that gets a little confusing. So in this discussion, I will use the term *instance* a bit more loosely. Just remember, when business people talk about real-world things, they're *not* talking about instances in a model(!).

Table 6–1. **Special-Purpose Elements of Structure.**

Special-Purpose Element of Structure	General Form	Example	Use in a Sample Business Rule Statement
categorization	(Class of thing₁) *is a category of* (class of thing₂).	'Corporate customer' *is a category of* 'customer'.	A customer is always considered corporate if the customer is not an individual person.
property	(thing₁) *has* (thing₂)	order *has* date taken order *has* date promised	An order's date promised must be at least 24 hours after the order's date taken.
composition (whole–part or partitive structure)	(whole) *is composed of* (parts) (part) *is included in* (whole)	chair *is composed of*: • legs • seat • back • armrests	A chair may be ordered without armrests.
classification	(Instance) *is classified as a* (class of thing).	Canada *is classified as a* country. Canadian dollar *is classified as a* currency.	An order may be priced using the currency 'Canadian dollar' only if the customer placing the order is located in Canada.

Categories and Categorizations

A category is a class of things whose meaning is more restrictive than, but otherwise compliant with, some other class of things. For example, *male* is a category of *person*. Each male is always a person, but not every person is a male. A male can have properties that would not apply to any person who is not a male. In general, a category represents a kind, or variation, within a more general concept.

> A category is a kind, or variation, of a more general concept.

Representing one class of things to be a category of another class of things is called *categorization*. A category is not the same as a role; unlike a role, its meaning is not completely tied up in any particular fact type. Figure 6–1 illustrates several categories (using heavy lines) building on the *briefing* example discussed in the previous Chapter.

Figure 6–1. Illustration of categories.

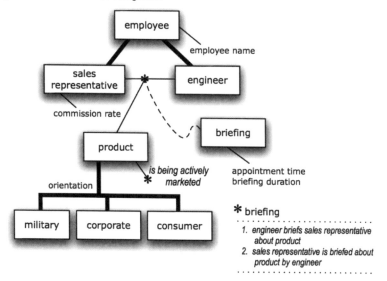

The following *categorizations* are illustrated by Figure 6–1.

- Both *sales representative* and *engineer* are recognized as categories of a more general concept *employee*. Note the property *employee name* is indicated for *employee*. Since all sales representatives and engineers can have names — indeed, *any* employee can — the *name* property is indicated only for *employee*. Remember that all sales representatives and engineers *are* employees in this business, so the *name* property pertains as a matter of

course to both *representative* and *engineer*. It does not need to be re-specified for them; inheritance of the property is assumed. On the other hand, commission rates apparently pertain only to sales representatives — not to all employees (e.g., not to engineers) — since *commission rate* is indicated only for *sale representative*.

- *Product* now has three categories — *military*, *corporate*, and *consumer* — forming a group. This group of categories is organized on the basis of a categorization scheme named *orientation* — more about that later. Note that (as always for categories) *military*, *corporate*, and *consumer* must be products. Indeed, unless everyone reading the diagram is thoroughly familiar with categorization, better labels would probably be *military product*, *corporate product*, and *consumer product*. The boxes represent that anyway, but these revised labels would emphasize the point.

> Be mindful of the more general concept
> in naming or interpreting a category.

Any category can have categories; any category of a category can have categories, and so on. Multiple levels of categorization are not uncommon in fact models. Indeed, such refinement or narrowing of meaning as you go 'deeper' yields a high degree of precision or selectivity for making statements about the business (e.g., giving business rules). For example, a business rule might be expressed for software engineers, a potential category of *engineer*, which does not apply either to other kinds of engineers or to employees in general.

Properties

MWUD defines *property* as *a quality or trait belonging to a person or thing*. Figure 6–1 indicates *employee name* to be a property of *employee*, and *commission rate* to be a property of *sales representative*. A thin line is used to attach each to the appropriate box (noun concept). Exactly what does the thin line represent?

- The thin line does *not* indicate that every member of a class of things actually has an instance of the property, only that it *can*. If each member of a class of things must have an instance of the property, an explicit business rule is required (e.g., *An employee must have an employee name.*).
- The thin line is actually a shorthand for a binary fact type. The wording for this binary fact type defaults to *(thing₁) has (thing₂)*. The important word here is *has*. The verb *to have* is very general — not specific or descriptive at all. *Has* makes very poor wording for fact types not specified as properties. For properties, on the other hand, a *has* default is often convenient.

> A property is a binary fact type in which one noun concept
> is closely tied to the meaning or understanding of another.

Can properties be worded using verbs other than *has*? *Yes.* For example, the *commission rate* property of *sales representative* might be worded *sales representative is compensated at commission rate*.

The property shown at the end of the line is often actually a role of some other noun concept. For example:

- Suppose commission rates are always percentages (in this business). Then the *commission rate* property of *sales representative* actually represents the fact type worded *sales representative is compensated at [commission rate] percentage*.

- Similarly, the *employee name* property of employee might actually represent the fact type worded *employee has [employee name] name*.

Note on Notation

Why bother with a graphical shorthand for properties? The answer has to do with scaling up. If you were to treat all properties as 'regular' fact types, the fact model would become hopelessly cluttered with connections having to do with such things as numbers, names, dates, units of measure, and much more. Such connections are of secondary importance to the business. Avoid that!

Figure 6–1 actually includes several other properties, as follows.

- Two properties for the objectification *briefing* have been indicated using a *single* thin line (another shorthand to reduce clutter).

- *Orientation*, which can be seen just above the crossbar for the categorization of *product,* is also a property, albeit a special kind. *Orientation* is the name of the *categorization scheme* used to organize the three kinds of product. Since *orientation* is a property of *product;* we can say *product has orientation*. (That's like saying *person has gender*, meaning *male* and *female*.) Is it required that every product fall into at least one of the three categories: *military, government,* or *consumer*? In other words, must every product have an orientation? (Or perhaps *exactly* one?) Don't assume so — that would require some explicit business rule(s).

Compositions — Whole–Part (Partitive) Structures

Many things in the real world are composites, made up of several other kinds of thing. For example, an automobile (simplistically) is composed of an engine, a body, and wheels. A mechanical pencil is made up of a barrel, a lead-advance mechanism, pencil lead, and eraser (from [ISO 704 2000], p. 9). An address (simplistically) is made up of a street number, a street, an apartment number, a city, a state/province, a country, and a zip code / postal code.

Sorting out the terminology and composition of such *whole–part* structures is often quite useful. Before looking at a graphical example, let's address some relevant questions:

- Is every instance of the whole in a whole–part structure required to have at least one instance of each part? *No.* For example, not every address has an apartment number. If every instance of the whole *is* required to have some part(s), an explicit business rule must be given.
- Can an instance of a whole have more than one instance of a kind of part? *Yes.* An automobile must have at least three wheels (a business rule). But use caution here. A whole–part structure usually works best where there is only one, or a small number of, each part.
- Can the specification of a whole–part structure indicate only one kind of part? *Yes.* However, exercise common sense! For example, is it really useful to consider the fact type worded *order includes line item* to be a whole-part structure? We do not favor that practice.
- Can a part itself be a whole composed of other parts? *Yes.* Multiple levels of composition are possible.
- Can both the whole and the parts be selectively involved in fact types on their own? *Yes.*
- Can an instance of a part exist independently from an instance of the whole? *Yes* (unless business rules disallow it). A wheel, for example, can be removed from an automobile.
- Can an instance of a part be in more than one instance of a whole at the same time? *Yes* (again, unless business rules disallow it). A power source, for example, can be part of more than one circuit.

> A whole-part structure permits
> capture of terms involved in composition.

Figure 6–2 illustrates a composition of *briefing* using a tree structure of thin lines to indicate the parts. The wording for this fact type, not shown explicitly, is assumed to be: *briefing is composed of: introduction, main body, conclusion.* In other words, *tell 'em what you're gonna to tell 'em, tell 'em, and tell 'em what you told 'em.*

Figure 6–2. Example of a composition (whole-part structure).

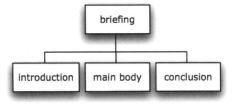

Classifications

A central focus in fact modeling is on identifying, defining, and naming the classes of things important to basic business operations. Most often the business cannot possibly know in advance what all the instances will be of a class of things. For example, most businesses cannot predict all their future customers.

For certain classes of things, however, the business can identify or prescribe in advance some or all of the instances, especially for those classes where the instances are relatively stable. For example, we know all the European countries at the present time. Moreover, the business will need to pre-define instances when it has some business rule(s) that pertain selectively to them — for example: *A shipment may be made only to the European countries United Kingdom or The Netherlands.*

Representing the connection between an instance and its particular class of things is called *classification* (or *assortment* in [SBVR 2007]). Figure 6-3 illustrates. The line with the double-wavy hatch mark indicates a classification connection from the class of things *European country* to some of its instances.

Note on Notation
The double-wavy hatch mark indicates that a meta level is crossed. To avoid clutter, we recommend ample use of neighborhoods to depict instance-level terminology.

Figure 6–3. Example of classification.

> European
> country

≈

    United Kingdom
    The Netherlands
    Germany
    Italy
    Switzerland

Some additional examples of classifications:

- *Health care:* All recognized health services — e.g., *consultation, office visit, hospital admission, surgery,* and so on.

- *Ship inspection:* All recognized parts of a ship — e.g., *bulkhead, hatch cover, railing, deck,* and so on.

These examples were chosen deliberately to illustrate that classifications can be multi-level. For example, the instances *bulkhead, hatch cover,* etc. of the class of things *ship part type* might themselves be viewed as classes of things with respect to *specific* bulkheads, hatch covers, etc. These specific bulkheads, hatch covers, etc. probably have serial numbers and would be found on a given ship or in a given shipyard. Business rules might be targeted toward any of these levels.

> A classification permits capture of an instance-level term.

Summary

Certain elements of structure useful for fact modeling come in handy, pre-defined shapes. This chapter has illustrated four of these special-purpose elements of structure: *properties, categorizations, compositions,* and *classifications.* These special connections between noun concepts extend the reach and precision of the fact model significantly. They also allow statements to be written with great precision — for example, giving business rules. Let's turn now to that.

Part 3

Business Rules

Chapter 7

Business Rules

Business rules apply to a broad spectrum of
needs. To illustrate, consider the following
situation that might occur in a baseball game.
Suppose it's the bottom of the seventh inning,
with two outs, two strikes on the batter, and
two base runners. The score is tied. The
batter is left-handed.

- One business rule might ensure the
  batter still gets only three strikes even if
  the pitcher is changed.
- Another business rule (or set of business rules) might compute the
  batter's hit percentage in similar prior circumstances.
- Yet another set of business rules might help choose the best relief
  pitcher.

Business rules cover all such needs, and more — all the kinds of guidance
needed for business operations. Understanding these kinds of guidance is a
'must'.

Fortunately, business rules fall into fundamental categories. In surveying
those categories, we will also look at non-rules (advices), guidelines,
exceptions, and more. A reminder — this treatment of business rules is
based on, and consistent with, SBVR.

What is a Business Rule?

A *business rule* is simply a rule that is under business jurisdiction. *Under
business jurisdiction* is taken to mean that the business can enact, revise,
and discontinue their business rules as they see fit. If a rule is not under
business jurisdiction in that sense, then it is not a business rule. For
example, the 'law' of gravity is obviously not a business rule. Neither are
the 'rules' of mathematics.

> A business rule is simply a rule
> under business jurisdiction.

The more basic question is the real-world, non-IT meaning of *rule*. Clearly, *rule* carries the sense of *guide for conduct or action* both in everyday life and in business. One way or another, this sense of *rule* can be found in most, if not all, authoritative dictionaries.

> A real-world rule serves as a guide for conduct or action.

If a rule is to serve as a guide for conduct or action, it must also provide the actual criteria for judging or evaluating that conduct or action. In other words, a rule serves as a *criterion* for making decisions. A business definition of *rule* therefore encompasses the sense of *criteria* as given by authoritative dictionaries.

> A real-world rule serves as a criterion for making decisions.

A rule always tends to remove a degree of freedom. If there were no rules, there would be complete freedom — i.e., anarchy. If some guidance is given but does not tend to remove some degree of freedom, it still might be useful, but it is not a rule per se. Such guidance is called an *advice*.

Figure 7–1 presents an overall categorization of guidance from the perspective of business people. All rules are either *behavioral* (also called *operative*) or definitional (also called *structural*). Use Figure 7–1 as a reference for the rest of this Chapter.

> A real-world rule always tends to remove a degree of freedom.

Figure 7–1. Categorization of business guidance.

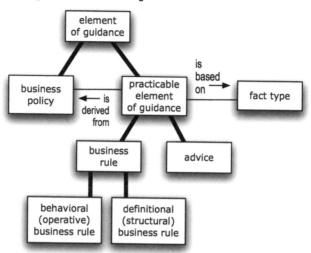

In contrast to a *business policy*, a business rule needs to be *practicable*. This means that a person who knows about a business rule could observe a relevant situation including his or her own behavior and decide directly whether or not the business was complying with the business rule. In general, a *business policy* is not practicable in that sense; a business policy must be interpreted into some more concrete business rule(s) that satisfy its supposed intent. (That's what the fact type in Figure 7–1 worded *practicable element of guidance is derived from business policy* is about.) For example the following business policy is not practicable: *Safety is our first concern.*

> A business rule must be practicable.

Just because business rules are practicable does *not* imply they are always automatable — many are *not*. For instance, consider the business rule: *A hard hat must be worn in a construction site.* Non-automatable rules need to be implemented within user activity. In many ways, managing non-automatable rules is even more difficult than managing automatable ones. They definitely have a place in your rulebook.

> Non-automatable rules should be managed too.

For a business rule (or an advice) to be practicable assumes that the business vocabulary on which it is based has been adequately developed, and has been made available as appropriate. Note the fact type in Figure 7-1 worded *practicable element of guidance is based on fact type.* Every business rule (and advice) should be directly based on a structured business vocabulary. Each business rule (and advice) is expressed using terms and wordings to create statements in building-block fashion.

Meaning vs. Statement

An additional, subtle point is this. The statement of a business rule is not actually the business rule; the *meaning* of the statement is the business rule. That's important because:

- The very same business rule (or advice) can be expressed by statements in different languages — e.g., French, Mandarin, etc. It's a global world these days!
- Even in the same language and the same notation (e.g., RuleSpeak), it's not uncommon to find a business rule (or advice) expressed in different ways by different people. That's a kind of redundancy you need to be able to discover and sort out.

In short, managing business rules needs to be about managing meaning — semantics — not just statements.

Behavioral Rules

Consider the business rule expressed as: *A gold customer must be allowed access to the warehouse.* Let's assume for now we don't need to consider any exceptions. Clearly this business rule can be violated. If a gold customer is denied access to the warehouse, then a violation has occurred. Presumably, some sanction is associated with such violation — for example, the security guard might be called on the carpet.

Any business rule that can be violated *directly* is a *behavioral rule.* (It doesn't matter whether it is automatable or not.) Behavioral rules are really *people* rules. Basic business operations typically involve significant numbers of behavioral rules.

> A business rule that can be violated directly is a behavioral rule.

Behavioral rules always carry the sense of *obligation* or *prohibition*. To reflect that sense, RuleSpeak prescribes the rule keywords *must* or *only* to express behavioral rules.

One way or another, behavioral business rules are always preventative, as the following examples illustrate.

- *Surgical gloves must be worn in performing surgery.*
  This business rule is intended to prevent infections.

- *A nurse must visit a patient at least every 2 hours.*
  This business rule is intended to prevent inattention to patients.

- *A gold customer must be allowed access to the warehouse.*
  This business rule is intended to prevent any denial of access.

Behavioral rules (also called *operative rules*) enable the business to run (i.e., to *operate*) its activities in a manner deemed suitable, optimal, or best aligned with its goals. Behavioral rules deliberately preclude specific possibilities (of *operation*) that are deemed undesirable, less effective, or potentially harmful. Behavioral rules remove those degrees of freedom. Often, sanction is real and immediate if a behavioral rule is broken.

Although the examples of behavioral rules above are not automatable, many can be automated. Here are some examples:

- *An order over $1,000 must not be accepted on credit without a credit check.*
- *A high-risk customer must not place a rush order.*
- *An order's date promised must be at least 24 hours after the order's date taken.*

Not Automatable?

Be careful about assuming a business rule can't be automated in some way. Sometimes, given the right technology (and sufficient business motivation) you might be surprised. Consider the business rule discussed earlier: *A person must wear a hard hat in a construction site.* You could use something like facial recognition software to determine whether a person is wearing a hardhat. If a person is not wearing one, the response could be to lock a gate the person needs to pass through or to trigger an alarm. Or put a GPS device on both the person and the hat. Don't underestimate technology!

Behavioral rules — *people rules* — are a distinctive feature of the business rules paradigm. All behavioral rules are business rules — people rules are always under business jurisdiction.

You may have noted that none of the examples of business rule statements given above (or anywhere in this book) use *if-then* syntax. A major reason is that if-then syntax is not well-suited for expressing behavioral rules. See sidebar.

Why Not *If-Then*?

Consider the business rule statement: *An employee must have a name.* What is the *then* of that? From a business perspective there is no *then*. There might be some enforcement if the rule is violated, but that's a different matter.

A typical IT counterpart might be: *If an employee does not have a name, then [do something].* The focus of this specification is not to express the rule, but rather to look for violations and do something in response. That focus is off-target for the primary business need.

In good English construction, every sentence has a subject. Although this subject may be implied or the sentence inverted, more often than not an explicit subject appears as the first word or phrase in the main body of the sentence. Such sentences are usually direct, and if well written, easy to follow. (The subject in the previous sentence, for example, is 'sentences'.)

So RuleSpeak does not use if-then syntax. It prescribes that statements of guidance always have an explicit subject at the beginning. That subject should be a noun, possibly qualified.

For additional discussion, see [Ross 2007].

Behavioral rules have fundamental implications in several areas:

- **Reasoning.** Since behavioral rules can be broken, they require special care in reasoning (automated or otherwise). Consider the behavioral rule: *A gold customer must be allowed access to the warehouse.* It cannot be assumed that the business rule has always been faithfully enforced; therefore, it cannot be inferred that in every situation where it was appropriate for a gold customer to be allowed access to the warehouse, the customer actually *was* allowed such access. Violations happen. Reasoning must be carefully restricted in this regard for behavioral rules.

- **Processes.** Behavioral rules have significant (and perhaps surprising) consequences for modeling processes. A key question in that regard is how the business *selectively* responds to violations of any particular business rule (if at all!). That question, in turn, raises the issue of how strictly each behavioral rule should be enforced — that is, its appropriate *level of enforcement.* I'll save that discussion for Chapter 12.

Definitional Rules

Additional business rules would be relevant to evaluating the behavioral rule: *A gold customer must be allowed access to the warehouse.* Specifically, what criteria should be used for determining whether a particular customer is *gold* or not? Here is an example: *A customer is always considered a gold customer if the customer places more than 12 orders during a calendar year.*

Such business rules are called *definitional rules.* Definitional rules always carry the sense of *necessity* or *impossibility.* To reflect that sense, RuleSpeak prescribes the rule keywords *always* or *never* to express a definitional rule.

Note to the Practitioner
Examples of definitional rules in this chapter and elsewhere in the book use the keywords *always* or *never* (or permissible variations) for clarity and emphasis. In current practice, distinguishing behavioral vs. definitional rules via selective keywords is not the greatest concern. For practical guidelines, refer to www.RuleSpeak.com.

Let's return to our two business rules. Suppose a customer appears at the warehouse, but the security guard is unaware of the criteria expressed in the definitional rule, or misapplies that criteria. Quite possibly the customer will not be given due access. The error, however, manifests itself as a violation of the behavioral rule, *not* the definitional rule per se. Definitional rules can be ill-conceived, misunderstood, or misapplied, but they cannot be directly violated.

> A definitional business rule can be ill-conceived, misunderstood, or misapplied, but it cannot be violated directly.

Unlike behavioral rules, not all definitional rules are business rules. The reason is that not all definitional rules are under business jurisdiction. As mentioned earlier, the 'law' of gravity is obviously not under business jurisdiction. Neither are the 'rules' of mathematics.

Evaluation of a *definitional rule* always classifies or computes something using all known facts. For example:

Classification Rule: *A customer is always considered a gold customer if the customer places more than 12 orders during a calendar year.*

Given any customer, evaluation of this definitional rule indicates whether the customer is or is not *gold* given all known facts.

> Computation Rule: *The total price of an order item is always computed as the product unit price times its quantity.*

Given any order item, evaluation of this definitional rule indicates the one result for *total price* that the known facts justify.

During business operations, definitional rules are used to evaluate 'where you are' — that is, the current state of affairs — as the need arises. For example:

- Is this customer a gold customer or not?
- Do we owe this customer a discount on this order?
- Does this patient have cat scratch fever or something else?

The result reached in each case is only as good as the decision logic given by the business rules. Poor or misapplied guidance yields poor or inconsistent results. In that case, some aspect of the knowledge 'breaks down' — it simply does not work properly.

Behavioral rules and definitional rules are fundamentally different. Disregard for behavioral rules leads to violations and possible sanctions; misapplication of definitional rules leads to miscalculations and off-base conclusions — but only indirectly, if at all, to violations.

If you are concerned about violations, you always need a behavioral rule. Consider the example of a definitional rule given earlier: *The total price of*

an order item is always computed as the product unit price times its quantity. Suppose a salesman decides to give a special volume discount to a personal friend. Again, the original business rule is merely for computing; it does not prohibit inappropriate conduct. For that, you would need a separate behavioral rule — for example: *A special volume discount may be given only to high-volume customers.*

For sets of definitional rules, you will often want to understand how their evaluation reaches particular results. More about that in the sidebar.

> Definitional rules are about how you organize — that is, *structure* — basic knowledge.

Logic Traces

Accurately evaluating (i.e., *reasoning over*) large numbers of definitional rules (automated or not) can produce unexpected or non-intuitive results. Often, the end-user or business analyst will want to ascertain *how* the results were produced — that is, to audit the way the logic was applied. Doing that requires starting with the results and tracing back through the chain of rules that led to the results.

Automated support for such *logic traces* is an important platform capability. A logic trace permits flaws and opportunities for improvement in decision logic to be identified. It also provides a means for less knowledgeable workers to learn about business know-how in hands-on fashion.

Definitional rules (also called *structural rules*) are about how the business organizes (i.e., *structures*) its basic knowledge. They give shape — i.e., *structure* — to core concepts of the business.

> A behavioral rule shapes business conduct;
> a definitional rule shapes business knowledge.

More Things You Should Know

Definitional Rules and Definitions

Definitional rules clearly contribute to the meaning of concepts. Obviously definitions do as well. In practice, can a clear distinction be maintained between definitions and definitional rules?

Yes. As discussed in Chapter 4, a good definition focuses on the essence of a concept — the core meaning of the concept to the business. Definitional rules, in contrast, indicate the exact lines of demarcation — that is, the precise 'edges' of the concept. Establishing these lines of demarcation are how definitional rules remove degrees of freedom.

For example, consider an 'essence' definition of *gold customer:* a customer that does a significant amount of business over a sustained period of time. Now compare that with the associated definitional rule: *A customer is always considered a gold customer if the customer places more than 12 orders during a calendar year.*

The definition expresses the fundamental notion about what *gold customer* means to the business or, more precisely, to business *people*. It is unlikely that basic notion will change — in other words, the notion as defined is very stable. That stability helps maintain continuity of knowledge within a community over time. It also aids in training newcomers, as well as in communicating with people outside the business area. In short, definitions should be aimed at *people*.

> **Note to the Practitioner**
> Aiming definitions toward people is our recommended best practice. It is supported but not required by SBVR.

> Definitions are for people.

The definitional rule, in contrast, gives precise criteria for determining whether a customer is or is not *gold* — criteria that quite possibly will change over time. Any aspect of business practice subject to change should be treated as a business rule, not embedded in definitions.

Another difference between definitions and definitional rules is that the latter frequently provide criteria that would not be so obvious from the definition, for example: *A customer is never considered a gold customer if the customer has been incorporated less than a year.*

Non-Rules (Advices)

Consider the statement: *A bank account may be held by a person of any age.* Although the statement certainly gives business guidance, it does not directly:

- Place any obligation or prohibition on business conduct. Therefore it does not express a behavioral rule.

- Establish any necessity or impossibility for knowledge about business operations. Therefore it does not express a definitional rule.

Because the statement removes no degree of freedom, it does not express a rule. Rather, it expresses something that is a non-rule — a.k.a. an *advice*.

Is it important then to write the advice down (i.e., capture and manage it)? *Maybe.* Suppose the statement reflects the final resolution of a long-standing debate in the company about how old a person must be to hold a bank account. Some say 21, others 18, some 12, and some say there should be no age restriction at all. Finally the issue is resolved in favor of no age restriction. It's definitely worth writing that down!

> An advice emphasizes what is possible or permissible as a matter of current business policy.

Now consider this statement: *An order $1,000 or less may be accepted on credit without a credit check.* This statement of advice is different. It suggests a business rule that possibly hasn't been captured yet: *An order over $1,000 must not be accepted on credit without a credit check.* Let's

assume the business needs this rule and considers it valid.

In that case you should write the *business rule* down — not the advice — because only the business rule actually removes any degree of freedom. Just because the advice says an order $1,000 or less may be accepted on credit without a credit check, that does not necessarily mean an order over $1,000 *must not.* A statement of advice only says just what it says.

Guidelines

Consider the behavioral rule: 'An order over $1,000 must not be accepted on credit without a credit check.' Suppose this behavioral rule is restated with a *should* instead of a *must* such that it reads: 'An order over $1,000 should not be accepted on credit without a credit check.' Now does it express an advice?

No. It is still a business rule, only with a lighter sense of prohibition. What actually changed was its presumed *level of enforcement.* Rather than strictly enforced, now the business rule has the sense: *It's a good thing to try to do this, but if you can't there's no sanction.* In other words, now it's simply a *guideline* (or *suggestion*, if you prefer).

> A guideline is a behavioral rule with no tangible enforcement.

Should you use *should* or *should not* (or similar forms) to express a lightly-enforced behavioral rule? *Not recommended.* In general, it's better to use consistent wording for all behavioral rules (e.g., *must* or *must not*). Remember, the level of enforcement for any given business rule often varies with changes in business practice. Guidance is one thing; level of enforcement is another — best not to mix the two! By the way, that's why you don't find *guideline* in Figure 7–1.

Two other things about guidelines:

- **Vocabulary.** A guideline for business operations — just like an advice or any other business rule for the same business — is expressed using the same underlying vocabulary. Note that in Figure 7–1 *all* elements of guidance *are based on* fact types. Let's put it this way: If you have the vocabulary to express your business rules, you already have the vocabulary you need to express any guideline.

- **Guidance Message.** Recall from Chapter 2 that a business rule statement *is* the guidance message. This remains true for guidelines. A guideline can indeed be violated, but no enforcement action is taken. Instead, the end user (if authorized) is simply informed. If you think of business rules simply as hard-and-fast constraints, you're missing an important part of the picture. In the larger sense, business rules are always about dispensing basic business knowledge in real time. Guidelines are an important part of that overall scheme.

Exceptions

No discussion of business rules would be complete without considering exceptions. To do the topic justice, however, requires a bit of groundwork. Let's examine the following two warehouse business rules:

Business Rule 1: *A gold customer must be allowed access to the warehouse.*

Business Rule 2: *A customer may have access to the warehouse only during regular business hours.*

Suppose some *gold* customer seeks access *after* regular business hours. Under that potential scenario we have a conflict.

A basic SBVR principle is that any guidance statement whose meaning conflicts with some other guidance statement(s) (or even some other part of the same statement) must be taken that way. In other words, if by taking some expression(s) literally you find that a potential conflict could arise, you are right — it can. You need to fix it. The principle is really about being able to fully trust what you read in front of you. If statements of business rules don't mean *literally* what they say, then can you really ever be sure what they do say!?

> You have to be able to trust
> what a statement of a business rule says.

So guidance statements should always be taken to mean exactly what they actually say — no more, no less. Potential conflicts such as the above must be resolved explicitly, within the actual statement(s). Several approaches that *don't* work in that regard include:

- Setting up some priority scheme to determine which 'wins'.
- Expressing some separate business rule(s) to determine which 'wins'.
- Deferring to some level of categorization to determine which 'wins' (e.g., A gold customer is a category of customer; therefore 'customer' rules 'win' over 'gold customer' rules).

To apply each business rule correctly under any of these approaches, sometimes you need to know more than just what a statement says. In other words, sometimes semantics are hidden, or at least external. Not good.

> If you understand the business vocabulary,
> you should never have to know more than exactly what a
> guidance statement says to fully understand it.

The only viable solution is that once a potential conflict is discovered, the guidance statement(s) that produce(s) that conflict need to be restated to avoid it. In other words, the statement(s) must *accommodate* the problematic circumstances. This guiding principle — the correct one for business communication — is called *Accommodation*.

So one of the warehouse business rules needs to be re-written. Which one? The answer depends entirely on business practice. Which of the following reworded versions might represent the correct or desired business practice?

> Reworded Business Rule 1: *A customer must be given access to the warehouse if the customer is a gold customer and the access is during business hours.*

> Reworded Business Rule 2: *A customer that is not a gold customer may have access to the warehouse only during business hours.*

Let's say the desired business practice is given by the second statement. So the two business rules jointly representing the correct business practices for warehouse access are:

> Business Rule 1: *A gold customer must be allowed access to the warehouse.*

> Business Rule 2: *A customer that is not a gold customer may have access to the warehouse only during business hours.*

Now we can finally address the issue of exceptions. Looking at the two resulting warehouse-access business rules ask yourself: *Which is an exception?!* Both? Neither? The formal answer is, once you *accommodate*, there really are no exceptions(!). There are just well-stated, fully-trustworthy business rules.

In conversation and other informal business communication, we often do talk about "exceptions" to business rules. For example we might say: *A customer may have access to the warehouse only during regular business hours.* Then later in the same conversation or message we might add: *By the way, none of what I've said applies to gold customers.*

Statements of business rules, however, should not be informal in that sense. You can never be sure when or where a statement might be read or what the context might be. So a business rule statement needs to express its full meaning. David Crystal, a noted world authority on language, explains things this way [Crystal 2005, p. 465]:

"When someone consults a reference book ... [in which] information is stored for future use, it is impossible to predict who is likely to use it ... There is no 'dialogue' element in the communication. The information has to be as self-contained as possible, for it is impossible to predict the demands which may one day be made on it, and in most cases there is no way in which the user can respond so as to influence the writer. Accordingly, when language is used for [such] purposes … it is very different from that used in everyday conversation — in particular, it displays a much greater degree of organization, impersonality, and explicitness."

Now I've never met or talked to David Crystal, but I'm confident I get his meaning.

> A business rule statement needs to express its full meaning. This principle is called *Wholeness*.

This principle of expressing the full meaning of each business rule is called *Wholeness*. Suppose your rulebook is deemed free of conflicts and you understand the business vocabulary correctly (two big *if's* of course). If your guidance statements are all expressed *wholly*, then:

- *Every statement is always self-explanatory.* No need to appeal to any other statement should ever arise in understanding the full meaning.
- *Every statement can always be taken at face value.* Take it out of conversational context and you can still trust exactly what it says.

By the way, there's a great deal a general rulebook system (GRBS) could do to simplify and condense *whole* statements for easier consumption — *if* it knew each worker's preferred conversational context. That would give you friendly *and* formal business communication.

> What you ultimately want is *friendly-and-formal* business communication.

Summary

Rule Independence is the key idea in business rules. The various principles underlying Rule Independence are enumerated in the *Business Rules Manifesto*, a copy of which can be found at the end of this book.

One consequence of Rule Independence is that business rules become an object of study and expertise in their own right — a new and exciting business competency. This chapter has outlined the fundamentals of that competency with a strong focus on the perspective of business people.

There is still more to come. The next step is to fully appreciate how business rules relate to events. Let's now turn to that important topic.

Chapter 8

Business Rules and Events: Flash Points

Intuitively, we know that certain business
rules apply when certain events occur. But
how exactly?

At the risk of stating the obvious, let me
begin by clarifying that a business rule and
an event are not the same thing. There
should be no confusion about that. A
business rule gives guidance; an event is
something that happens (MWUD – *event* 1a.)

Multiple Events for Each Business Rule

How do business rules and events relate? Consider the business rule: *A
customer must be assigned to an agent if the customer has placed an order.*
Figure 8–1 shows the relevant terms and wordings for this business rule
statement.

Figure 8–1. Terms and Wordings for the Agent-Assignment Business Rule.

The business rule itself has been expressed in declarative manner. This
means, in part, that it does not indicate any particular process, procedure, or
other means to enforce or apply it. It is simply a
business rule — nothing more, nothing less.

Declarative also means that the business rule
makes no reference to any event where it
potentially could be violated or needs to be
evaluated. The business rule does not say, for
example, "*When* a customer places an order,
then...."

This observation is extremely important for the following reason. *"When a customer places an order" is not the only event when the business rule could potentially be violated.* Actually, there is another event when this business rule could be violated: *"When* an agent leaves our company...." This other event could pose a violation of the business rule under the following circumstances: (a) The agent is assigned to a customer, and (b) that customer has placed at least one order.

In other words, the business rule could potentially be violated during *two* quite distinct kinds of events. The first — *"When* a customer places an order ..." — is rather obvious. The second — *"When* an agent leaves our company ..." — might be much less so. Both events are nonetheless important because either could produce a violation of the business rule.

This example is not atypical or unusual in any way. In general, *every* business rule (expressed in declarative form) produces two or more kinds of events where it could potentially be violated or needs to be evaluated. (I mean *produces* in the sense of *can be analyzed to discover.*) We call these events *flash points*. Business rules do exist that are specific to an individual event (more on that in a minute), but they represent the exception, rather than the general case.

> A business rule generally produces two or more
> events — *flash points* — where it needs to be evaluated.

Let's summarize what I've said so far:

- Business rules and events, while related, are not the same.
- Specifying business rules declaratively helps ensure no flash point is missed.
- Any given business rule needs to be evaluated for potentially multiple flash points. Figures 8–2 and 8–3 provide additional examples to reinforce this crucial insight.

Figure 8–2. Multiple Events for a Simple Business Rule.

Business Rule: *A customer must have an address.*

Flash Points:

Event #1: *When an attempt occurs to assert the existence of a new customer.*

Event #2: *When an attempt occurs to eliminate the address of a customer.*

Figure 8–3. Multiple Events for a More Complex Business Rule.

Business Rule: *A territory must not include more than one of the following:*
*   * Non-candidate traditional gas station,*
*   * Ultra-service,*
*   * Food outlet.*

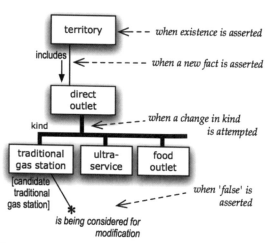

Flash Points:

Event #1: *When an attempt occurs to assert the existence of a new territory.*

Event #2: *When an attempt occurs to include a direct outlet in a territory.*

Event #3: *When an attempt occurs to change the kind of a direct outlet already included in a territory.*

Event #4: *When an attempt occurs to assert that a traditional gas station already included in a territory is not being considered for modification.*

Why is that insight so important? *The two or more events where a business rule needs to be evaluated are likely to occur within at least two, and possibly many, different processes, procedures, or use cases.* Yet for all these different processes, procedures, and use cases, there is only a *single* business rule. By unifying the business rule, and faithfully supporting all its flash points wherever they occur, you ensure consistent decisions across all the processes, procedures, and use cases.

> By faithfully supporting all flash points for a business rule wherever they occur, you ensure consistent decisions across all processes, procedures, and use cases.

Discovering and analyzing flash points for business rules often also proves a very useful activity in validating business rules. Important and sometimes surprising guidance issues (a.k.a. business policy questions) often crop up. This capability is one of many for validation and verification of business rules that a general rulebook system (GRBS) can and should support.

> Your general rulebook system (GRBS) should automatically identify all flash points for each business rule as part of validation.

This type of business-rule-centric event analysis is not a feature of *any* traditional IT methodology. Once you fully appreciate that point, you can begin to see why legacy systems so often produce such inconsistent results.

CRUD Events

CRUD stands for create, retrieve, update, delete — all *system* events. You should never express business rules based on CRUD. For one thing, CRUD isn't business terminology so the result will always be a data or system rule rather than a business rule. Not good!

But there's more. Using CRUD to express rules has hidden side effects. Often the result is an unintended or unknowing limiting of coverage to a single event. Let's work through an example:

CRUD Rule: *Update product cost if the cost of any of the product's components changes.*

In RuleSpeak, the subject of any business rule statement providing a computation formula is always the name of what is being computed. *Product's cost* is therefore indicated as the subject in the following revised version.

Business Rule: *A product's cost must be computed as the sum of the cost of all the product's components.*

The original CRUD version for this business rule limits coverage to a single flash point — *when* the cost of a component included in a product changes. The revised version covers not only that flash point, but the following two as well:

- *When* a component is newly added to the make-up of a product.
- *When* a component is newly removed from the make-up of a product.

This broadening of coverage should be analyzed carefully, of course — it might not represent true business intent. (If not, the *when* condition should appear explicitly in the RuleSpeak version at the end of the sentence.) My point is this: CRUD is simply a *when* condition in technical garb. *No when condition, especially a disguised one, should ever appear in a business rule statement accidentally.*

No <u>when</u> condition should ever appear
in a business rule statement accidentally.

Let's consider another example:

CRUD Rule: *Don't <u>delete</u> a customer that has placed any open orders.*

What is the true business intent of this rule? It stands to reason that if deleting a customer that has placed an open order is disallowed, then *opening* an order *without* a customer is probably also disallowed. From a business perspective, always knowing who the customer is for any open order is probably key. Removing the CRUD produces:

Business Rule: *An open order must be placed by a customer.*

This revised version omits any mention of the *delete a customer* flash point. It inherently also covers the *open an order* flash point (i.e., asserting that an order is open). Even this simplest possible business rule turns out to have more than one flash point!

In RuleSpeak, *when* is always taken to mean *only at the point in time that some specified event occurs.* Suppose the business rule above had been written this way (not recommended):

Rule: <u>*When*</u> *an order is created, it must have a promised shipment date.*

In this version, the rule applies only *when* an order is created (comes into existence). But what about two seconds later?! Should anybody (or any system) be allowed to delete (discard) the promised shipment date? *Probably not!*

Including a *when* clause in the expression of a business rule chains the business rule to that specific flash point. More often than not, that narrowing of coverage does not reflect true business intent. Experience has shown that the large majority of business rules are inherently and naturally multi-flash-point. Be very careful when you say *when*!

> Including a <u>when</u> clause in the expression of a business rule chains it to that specific flash point.

Summary

The large majority of business rules have multiple flash points — events when they need to be evaluated. These flash points are inherent to any business rule expressed declaratively. No flash point should ever be mentioned in stating a business rule unless first verified as specifically expressing business intent.

Separation of business rules from events, another aspect of Rule Independence, has many benefits including:

Agility: Each business rule can be specified declaratively and *in one place*. One-place specification (*single-sourcing*) means the business rule will be easier to find — and easier to change quickly.

Consistency: Unification of each business rule across all its flash points ensures consistency in making decisions across all processes that produce those events. Better for the processes; better for the decisions!

Chapter 9

The Art of Business Rules

A consequence of Rule Independence
is that business rules become an object
of analysis and expertise in their own
right — a new and exciting business
competency. This chapter surveys
several key skills needed for that
new competency.

Business Rule Reduction

When business rules are first captured, they often embed multiple criteria
that need to be broken out as separate business rules. Breaking them out is
called *rule reduction*. The goal is to produce easily-understood, highly-
granular expressions of business guidance that can be independently re-used
and modified.

> The goal of *rule reduction* is to produce easily-understood,
> highly-granular expressions of business guidance
> that can be independently re-used and modified.

To briefly illustrate, consider the following computation business rule:

Starting-Point Business Rule: *The total price
of an order item is always computed as the
product unit price times its quantity minus
10% if the order is the first order ever placed
by the customer.*

To reduce complexity, a good first step is to break out any computations as separate business rules. As a result:

> Business Rule 1 (Definitional): *The first-time discount is always computed as 10% times the total price of an order item.*

Be alert for any more general concept(s) not mentioned by the original statement that might apply. For example, the first-time discount is perhaps just one of many discounts that sometimes might be *applicable* to order items. As a result:

> Business Rule 2 (Definitional): *The first-time discount is always considered an applicable discount for each order item of the first order that a customer places.*

Restate the starting-point business rule using new terms such as *applicable discount*. The result is always a simpler statement:

> Business Rule 3 (Definitional): *The total price of an order item is always computed as the product unit price times its quantity, minus applicable discounts.*

Business Rule Quality

Determining the quality of business rules — their *fitness* — is not an IT issue; it's primarily a business one. You want to ensure quality *before* business rules are translated into any implementation language or deployed into actual business operations. Your worst-case scenario is detecting anomalies live! The earlier you detect them, the better (and the cheaper!). The goal is to pursue business rule quality directly and proactively.

> The earlier you detect anomalies in business rules,
> the better — and the cheaper!

Assessing the quality of business rules falls into two general areas: *validation* and *verification*.

Validation means ensuring the correctness of business rules with respect to business purpose. You want to make certain that, when applied, the results will be appropriate in all relevant circumstances. Validation is largely a matter of human inspection, but a general rulebook system (GRBS) can assist in certain ways:

- Diagrams can depict logical or computational dependencies between business rules.

- Test scenarios can be retained so prior results can be compared with new results for modified rule sets.
- Each business rule can be analyzed to identify all flash points, to help ensure its logic is complete and robust.

> Rule validation is about whether
> you have the *right* business rules.

Verification means assessing fitness with respect to logical consistency. Verification involves discovering business rules (usually two or more in combination) that exhibit some anomaly. Below is a quick sampler of common anomalies, along with simple examples. Can you figure out what's going on in each case?

Linguistic Equivalence
- *A permanent employee must receive a salary.*
- *An employee who is permanent must receive a salary.*

Modal Equivalence
- *An order over $1,000 must not be accepted on credit without a credit check.*
- *An order over $1,000 may be accepted on credit only with a credit check.*

Logical Equivalence
- *A high-risk customer must not place a rush order.*
- *A rush order must not be placed by a high-risk customer.*

Subsumation
- *A rush order must have a destination.*
- *An order must have a destination.*

Outright Conflict
- *A high-priced, fragile item must be picked up by the customer.*
- *A high-priced, fragile item must be shipped by an insured carrier.*

Potential Conflict
- *A shipment must include more than 1 order.*
- *An out-of-state shipment may include only 1 order.*

> Rule verification is about whether your business rules are *right*.

Business rules will be captured by different people at different points in time, so anomalies can appear even in the best-coordinated efforts. By the way, such anomalies are not the result of Rule Independence; rather, independent expression of business rules in declarative form simply makes the anomalies much easier to find. Fortunately, detection of many anomalies can be automated. There is only one caveat, but it's a big one: *You must coordinate the business vocabulary used to express the business rules.*

> Your general rulebook system (GRBS) should provide analysis tools directly addressing business rule quality.

An additional area of concern in business rule quality is the *completeness* of business rules — that is, whether there are gaps or holes in coverage. As a simple example, consider this statement of advice: *An order $1,000 or less may be accepted on credit without a credit check.* A missing business rule might be: *An order over $1,000 must not be accepted on credit without a credit check.*

Decision Tables

As you scale up, having an effective means to visualize and manage entire *sets* of business rules at a time becomes ever more important. Decision tables are an excellent tool for that. In general, decision tables can be used where three criteria are met. These sound more difficult than they really are.

1. A significant number of rules are parallel — that is, they share the same subject, have exactly the same evaluation term(s), and are equivalent (but not identical) in effect. In other words, the business rules all share a common pattern and purpose.

2. Each evaluation term has a finite number of relevant instances or collections of instances. Collections of instances are usually represented as ranges of values — a.k.a. *brackets*.

3. Given the different instances or brackets of the evaluation term(s), the outcomes cannot be predicted by a single formula. (If a single formula could predict the outcomes, using a single business rule or set of business rules to give the unified formula is a better approach.)

> Decision tables represent sets of business rules.

Here is a simple example involving eight business rules:

1. Applicable sales tax is to be 6.0% if year = 1999.
2. Applicable sales tax is to be 6.5% if year = 2000.
3. Applicable sales tax is to be 6.5% if year = 2001.
4. Applicable sales tax is to be 6.5% if year = 2002.
5. Applicable sales tax is to be 6.25% if year = 2003.
6. Applicable sales tax is to be 7.0% if year = 2004.
7. Applicable sales tax is to be 8.0% if year = 2005.
8. Applicable sales tax is to be 8.15% if year = 2006.

Note that this set of business rules satisfies all three criteria above:

1. The eight business rules are exactly parallel. They share the same subject, *applicable sales tax*; have exactly the same evaluation term, *year*; and are equivalent (but not identical) in effect, an indicated *sales tax percentage* for each given year.

2. The evaluation term, *year*, has a finite number of relevant instances (eight).

3. The outcomes — the percentages indicated for *applicable sales tax* — cannot be predicted by a formula.

> Decision tables are an excellent means
> to visualize and manage parallel business rules.

The following business rule statement and associated decision table shows the consolidated decision logic for the eight business rules above. I think you'll agree it's quite an improvement!

Business Rule:
Applicable sales tax is to be the percent value in the Sales Tax by Year Table for a given year.

Sales Tax by Year Table

Year	Applicable Sales Tax
1999	6.0
2000	6.5
2001	6.5
2002	6.5
2003	6.25
2004	7.0
2005	8.0
2006	8.15

Decision tables are also useful for finding missing business rules — that is, for assessing the *completeness* of a set of business rules. For example, if any cell in a decision table has nothing in it, that outcome is possibly missing and probably should be addressed. I'll come back to the issue of completeness later.

The decision table above has only a single evaluation term. Most decision tables have more than that. To illustrate, the following revised business rule and decision table adds a second evaluation term *county* to determine *applicable sales tax*.

Business Rule: *Applicable sales tax is to be the percentage in the Sales Tax by Year and County Table for a given year and county.*

Sales Tax by Year and Country Table

County

Year	Harkin	Lopes	Qwan	Quail
1999	6.95	8.2	7.35	4.0
2000	6.73	8.3	9.0	4.5
2001	6.15	8.4	9.0	5.0
2002	6.15	8.3	9.0	5.5
2003	6.15	8.4	6.75	6.0
2004	6.15	8.2	6.75	6.75
2005	5.75	8.2	6.75	7.0
2006	5.95	8.4	7.5	7.25

Representing *more* than two evaluation terms using a two-dimensional media (e.g., paper) becomes problematic. If there are three or more evaluation terms, but all but two (or fewer) are simple, the decision logic can still be represented in variations of a two-dimensional format. (Think tax tables.) An example of *simple* would be *is income taxable?* which can be answered by only *yes* or *no*. Such variations might use:

- Split rows or columns within a single array.

- Multiple arrays, with one array per relevant instance or bracket of one (or more) of the evaluation terms.

Beyond that, automated support by a general rulebook system (GRBS) or other tool becomes indispensable. The following business rule and associated decision table illustrates.

Business Rule: *The delivery method for an order is to be as in the Delivery Method Table.*

Delivery Method Table

Delivery Method for an Order

Decision Criteria	Picked Up by Customer	Shipped by Normal Service	Shipped by Premium Service
Rush order	No	Yes	Yes
Order includes fragile item	No	Yes	—
Order includes specialty item	No	No	—
Order includes high-priced item	No	No	—
Order includes item involving hazardous materials	No	Yes	Yes
Category of customer	Silver	Gold	Platinum
Destination of order	—	Local	Remote

The Delivery Method Table establishes the basis for determining the delivery method for an order. Three possible delivery methods (the outcomes) are indicated along the top. Seven decision criteria appear at the left as labels for the rows. (Since some are logical expressions, *decision criteria* is more appropriate than *evaluation terms*.) This table therefore involves seven dimensions.

Six of the decision criteria are binary (*yes, no* or *local, remote*), whereas one, *category of customer*, involves three possibilities (*silver, gold, platinum*). The choice of delivery method for an order depends on what appears in all the cells of a column. A dash (—) in a cell indicates that the associated decision criteria does not matter in determining the outcome; that is, *any* alternative for that decision criteria will produce the same outcome.

> Special analyses can be performed automatically for decision tables to ensure business rule quality and completeness.

Decision tables with three or more non-simple dimensions are unavoidably complex, so they must be developed with special care. As always, the issue of completeness is also important. How complete is the sample decision table above? *Not very!* Can you tell why? The answer is worked out on the next page.

Answer to the Delivery Method Table Completeness Question

The completeness of the decision table can be calculated as follows:

(1) The total number of *possible* combinations for the instances of the seven decision criteria can be calculated as: $2^6 \times 3 = 192$. This calculation reflects the fact that six of the decision criteria apparently have two alternatives each (*yes* and *no* for five of them, and *local* and *remote* for the other), whereas the seventh (category of customer) apparently has three (*silver*, *gold*, and *platinum*).

(2) The total number of combinations *actually represented* in the table can be determined as follows. Column 2 represents one combination — each cell has something in it. Columns 1 and 3 are a bit more complicated because they both have one or more cells with dashes, indicating acceptance of any alternative — for example, either *yes* or *no*. Column 1 includes one such cell, so that column actually provides the basis for establishing the outcome for *two* combinations — one if the cell had *local* and one if it had *remote*. Column 3 includes three such cells, so that column actually establishes the basis for 2^3 or 8 outcomes. Altogether, the decision table actually establishes the basis for establishing 11 outcomes $(2 + 1 + 8 = 11)$.

(3) Having determined how many combinations the decision table actually addresses (11), we can now determine how many it does not: $192 - 11 = 181$. So some 181 possible combinations have not been addressed at all! We must therefore conclude this decision table is *not very complete*.

Summary

A consequence of Rule Independence is that business rules become an object of analysis and expertise in their own right — a new and exciting business competency. This chapter briefly surveyed three key skills needed for that new competency: *business rule reduction, business rule quality,* and *decision tables*.

Part 4

Enterprise Design

Chapter 10

Smart Architectures and the Point of Knowledge

Let's stand back and take a look at some very big questions. What do business rules offer enterprise design? How should you think about business vocabularies (semantics) and business rules in the context of enterprise architectures and software design? Where do you want your company to be headed in retaining, managing, and deploying its fundamental know-how? How do you get your company to the *point of knowledge*?

When you start to fully understand business rules, a whole lot of other pieces of the puzzle fall right into place. You arrive at *smart architectures,* which gives you *smart knowledge management* and *smart processes.* This Chapter explains.

The Point of Knowledge

For me, the *point of knowledge* (POK) is a real place. POK is where elements of know-how for business operations are developed, applied, assessed, and ultimately retired. In other words, POK is where business rules happen. Knowledge is power, so you can also think about POK as point of *empowerment.*

> The point of knowledge is a real place.

POK corresponds to point of sale (POS) in the world of commerce. POK and POS are similar in several ways:

- In both, something is exchanged. In POS, it's goods. In POK, it's knowledge — the know-how of business operations.

- In the world of commerce, we often say that consumer and supplier are *parties* in point-of-sale events. Each of us is a consumer in some point-of-sale events, and many of us act as suppliers in others. The same is true for POK. Each of us is a consumer of know-how in some POK events, and many of us act as suppliers in others. Sometimes we switch roles within minutes or even seconds.

- A well-engineered experience at the point of sale has obvious benefits both for the consumer — a positive buying experience — and for the business of the supplier — real-time intelligence about sales volume, cash flow, buying trends, inventory depletion, consumer profiles, etc. A well-engineered experience at the POK likewise has obvious benefits. For the consumer, it means a positive *learning* experience. For the business of the supplier, benefits include real-time intelligence about the 'hit' rate of business rules, patterns of evolving consumer (and supplier) behavior, emergence of compliance risks, etc.

> A well-engineered POK produces a positive learning experience
> for business consumers of knowledge.

The consumer/supplier experience at the POK is crucial to worker productivity and job satisfaction. In no small measure, optimizing this experience is the real challenge in POK engineering. And it must be deliberate. After all, what's exchanged at the POK is know-how — something you can't carry around in your hands.

> What's exchanged at the POK is know-how — something you
> can't carry around in your hands.

Nonetheless, your company's know-how is very real. What do I mean by *know-how*? MWUD says:

Know-how: *accumulated practical skill or expertness ... especially: technical knowledge, ability, skill, or expertness of this sort*

Today, much of your know-how is tacit — lose the people, you lose the know-how. How can you avoid that? Make the know-how *explicit* as business rules. The POK is how you make that happen.

Critical success factors in engineering an effective POK include:

- All communication must be strictly in the language of the business, not IT.

- All interaction must be gauged to the knowledge level (and authorization) of each individual party.

- Less-experienced parties playing the consumer role must be enabled to perform as closely as possible at the level of the company's most experienced workers.

- Basic business know-how — business rules — must be presented and applied in a succinct, highly-selective fashion.

- Basic business know-how — business rules — must also be presented and applied in a *timely* fashion (i.e., 'just-in-time') to accommodate fast-paced refinement and change in business policies and practices.

Point-of-Knowledge Architecture

Let me use an example to sketch the workings of business rules in smart architecture. Refer to Figure 10–1 to visualize how the system works.

Figure 10–1. Point of Knowledge Architecture (POKA).

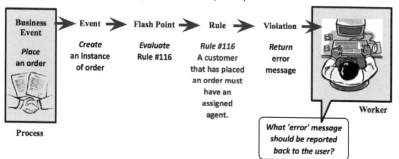

Suppose you have a process or procedure that can be performed to take a customer order.

- An order is received. Some kind of event occurs in the system. It doesn't really matter too much what kind of event this is; let's just say the system becomes aware of the new order.

- The event is a flash point — one or more business rules pertain to it. One is: *A customer that has placed an order must have an assigned agent.*

- We want real-time compliance with business policy, so this business rule is evaluated immediately for the order. Again, it doesn't much matter what component in the system does this evaluation; let's just say some component, service, or platform knows how.

- Suppose the customer placing the order does *not* have an assigned agent. The system should detect a fault, a violation of the business rule. In other words, the system should become aware that the business rule is not satisfied by this new state of affairs.

- The system should respond immediately to the fault. In lieu of any smarter response, at the very least it should respond with an appropriate message to someone, perhaps to the order-taker (assuming that worker is authorized and capable).

What exactly should the error message say?

Obviously, the message can include all sorts of 'help'. But the most important thing it should say is what kind of fault has occurred from the business perspective. In other words, it should start off simply by literally saying, *"A customer that has placed an order must have an assigned agent."* We say the error message (or preferably guidance message) *is* the business rule statement.

That's a system putting on a smart face, a knowledge-friendly face, at the very point of knowledge. But it's a two-way street. By flashing business rules in real-time, you have an environment perfectly suited to rapidly identifying opportunities to evolve and improve business practices. The know-how gets meaningful mindshare. That's a ticket to continuous improvement and true agility.

> Smart architecture offers continuing opportunities
> to evolve and improve business rules.

Smarter and Smarter Responses

Is it enough for the system simply to return a business rule statement as the guidance message and stop there? Can't it do more? *Of course.*

For the order-taking scenario, a friendly system would immediately offer the user a means to correct the fault (again assuming the user is authorized and capable). Specifically, the system should offer the user another
procedure, pulled up instantaneously, to assign an appropriate agent. If successful, the user could then move on with processing the order.

This smart approach knits procedures together just-in-time based on the flash points of business rules. It dynamically supports highly-variable patterns of work, always giving pinpoint responses to business events (not system events). In short, it's exactly the right approach for process models wherever applying know-how is key — which these days, is just about everywhere!

> Smart architecture knits procedures together just-in-time
> based on the flash points of business rules.

The *Business Rules Manifesto* says this: "Rules define the boundary between acceptable and unacceptable business activity." If you want dynamic processes, you must know exactly where that boundary lies, and how to respond to transgressions (at flash points) in real time.

Is that as smart as processes can get? Not yet. Over time, the business rules for assigning appropriate agents might become well enough understood to be captured and made available to the
system. Then when a fault occurs, the system can evaluate the business rules to assign an agent automatically. At that point, all this knowledge

work gets tucked very neatly under the covers. Even if the business rules you can capture are sufficient for only routine assignments, you're still way ahead in the game.

Smart architecture based on business rules is unsurpassed for *incremental* design, where improvement:

- Focuses on real business know-how, not just better GUIs or dialogs.

- Continues vigorously after deployment, not just during development.

- Occurs at a natural business pace, not constrained to software release cycles.

The *Manifesto* says it this way: "An effective system can be based on a small number of rules. Additional, more discriminating rules can be subsequently added, so that over time the system becomes smarter." That's exactly what you need for knowledge retention, as well as to move pragmatically toward the knowledge economy. Business rules give you *true* agility.

> A smart architecture based on business rules
> is unsurpassed for incremental design.

Smarter and Smarter Workers

Now let's talk about smart architecture from a consumer point of view. What people-challenges face your business today? What role should business systems play?

Time shock. As the rate of change accelerates, workers are constantly thrust into new roles and responsibilities. They must be guided through unfamiliar procedures or business know-how as thoroughly and as efficiently as possible. The business pays a price, either directly or indirectly, if getting workers up to speed is too slow (or too painful). Time shock is like culture shock — very disorienting if you're not prepared for rapid immersion.

> Time shock is like culture shock — very disorienting
> if you're not prepared for rapid immersion.

Training. The flip side of time shock is training — *how* to get workers up to speed. Training is expensive and time-consuming. Yet as the rate of change accelerates, more and more (re)training is required. Where do you turn for solutions?

The foremost cause of time shock for business workers is rapid change in the business rules. At any given time, workers might be found at virtually any stage of time shock. Sometimes, you might find them completely up-to-speed, other times completely lost. Most of the time, they are probably somewhere in between. That poses a big challenge with respect to training.

The only approach to training that will truly scale is on-the-job self-training. That requires smart architecture, where pinpoint know-how can be put right in front of workers in real time as the need arises — that is, right at the point of knowledge. What that means, in effect, is that the relevant portion of the company's know-how — its rulebook — is 'read' to the worker on-line, right as the worker bumps up against the business rules.

So a key idea in the business rules paradigm is that operational business systems must become *knowledge companions* for workers in the knowledge economy. After all, isn't making *people* smarter the whole point of knowledge?!

> Business systems must become knowledge companions
> for workers in the knowledge economy.

Summary

The point of knowledge is a real place. POK is where know-how of business operations is developed, applied, assessed, and ultimately retired. In other words, POK is where business rules happen.

In smart architectures, business systems become knowledge companions, enabling never-ending, on-the-job training. Flash points of knowledge — real-time evaluation of business rules — enables dynamic processes and personalized, just-in-time delivery of completely up-to-date business guidance.

A smart architecture is one equipped to address the formidable challenges facing businesses today — the accelerating rate of change, massive customization, and products and services that are ever richer in knowledge. Effective engineering of the POK is the new litmus test for agility.

> Effective engineering of the POK is
> the new litmus test for agility.

Chapter 11

Business Rules and Business Processes

Many companies today are looking to manage business activity on more of a beginning-to-end, value-add basis. That requires thinking cross-organizationally, always keeping to the business perspective. Can business rules help? Yes, greatly. This chapter explains.

How Business Rules Relate to Business Processes

Just in case I need to say this, yes, you still need business process models when you do business rules. Business rules do not substitute for business processes, they just make them a lot better.

The best definition of *business process* I have found to date is Janey Conkey Frazier's: *the tasks required for an enterprise to satisfy a planned response to a business event from beginning to end with a focus on the roles of actors, rather than the actors' day-to-day job.*

What do business rules do for business processes? Roger Burlton says it this way: "If you separate the business rules, you can develop remarkably stable business processes." If you're looking to manage business activities on a business-process basis, stability is key. Burlton goes on to say: "The really rapid change is in the business rules ... *not* in the business processes." *Right!*

> The really rapid change is in the business rules,
> *not* the business processes.

How do business rules and business processes relate? Burlton observes that business processes "… transform inputs into outputs *according to guidance* — policies, standards, rules, etc.…" The key phrase in that is *according to guidance.* Guidance is exactly what business rules provide. Let's take a closer look, first focusing on definitional rules.

Definitional Rules and Business Processes

The relationship of definitional rules and business processes is a direct one. Definitional rules simply off-load work pertaining to knowledge. They do so in two basic ways:

Computation: Computation rules provide decision logic needed to perform calculations.

Classification: Classification rules provide decision logic needed to determine whether or not something is true. See sidebar.

About Classification

Technically, determining whether something is true or not means deciding whether something does or does not fall into some particular class of things — hence, *classification*. For example, does this patient have cat scratch fever? In other words, does this patient's case fall into the cat-scratch-fever class of things? As this example illustrates, classification rules are directly relevant to the general problem (not just medical) of *case management*.

For either computation or classification, decision logic can become quite complex involving many business rules. Trying to capture all those business rules within the 'flow' of a business process model is frankly hopeless.

> Trying to capture business rules within the 'flow'
> of a business process model is hopeless.

Instead, you should reference or invoke decision logic indirectly. That can occur in at least two basic ways:

- *Via the name of a task.* For example, in insurance you might see a task called 'Adjudicate Claim'. This task requires a decision to be made, which in turn requires definitional rules.
- *Via the expression of a conditional flow.* For example, in insurance you might see conditional flows such as 'if claim is complete' or 'if fraud is suspected'. These conditions also indicate decisions to be made; again definitional rules are required.

Perhaps the most serious mistake people make in modeling business processes is including series of binary decision points ('diamonds') where flows branch based on *yes-or-no* (Boolean) logic. What's wrong with that? For one thing, many business decisions (most?) aren't binary(!). For another, the business process model quickly

becomes so detailed and cluttered, you'll lose sight of the business value-add. Good communication and business buy-in will fade fast.

Quite often what people are actually trying to do when they embed a series of diamonds in their business process models is to capture and represent decision logic (read *business rules*). Burlton characterizes that practice this way: "Anytime you stick diamonds in your business process model you're dead." Call it a *worst* practice.

> Sticking diamonds in your business process model
> is a *worst* practice.

Behavioral Rules and Business Processes

Behavioral rules are ones that *people* could violate. In a game of football, behavioral rules are why you need referees on the field during each game — someone to watch and intervene if any violations occur. Behavioral rules, which arise any time people could be involved (not just knowledge), are a distinctive feature of the business rules paradigm.

> Behavioral rules arise any time
> people could be involved in a business process.

Ways in which behavioral rules relate to business process models are sometimes focused and direct, and sometimes not. Here are some sample concerns that behavioral rules address:

Iteration. Business processes often include loops that permit iteration. Timing and repetition criteria for these loops can be expressed as business rules, for example:

Maximum time allowed between iterations.

Behavioral Rule: *Additional information needed for a claim must be requested at least every 5 days if not received.*

Minimum time allowed between iterations.

Behavioral Rule: *Additional information needed for a claim must not be requested more often than every 24 hours.*

Maximum iterations permitted.

Behavioral Rule: *The total number of requests made for additional information needed for a claim must not exceed 10.*

Maximum time permitted for completion.

Behavioral Rule: *A request for additional information needed for a claim must not be made after 10 days.*

Service Level Agreements. A service level agreement generally involves four things: (1) an action item, (2) a party, (3) escalation criteria, and (4) timing criteria.

Behavioral Rule: *A customer service request must be brought to the attention of a supervisor if the request is not resolved within 4 hours.*

In this example we find: (1) the action item *customer service request*, (2) the party *supervisor*, (3) the escalation criteria *if not resolved*, and (4) the timing criteria *within 4 hours*.

Compliance. A business process can involve hundreds of business rules (or more!) addressing specific things *people* need to do to comply with business policy or external regulation. For example: *A customer that has placed an order must have an assigned agent.* A business process cannot possibly address that many business rules directly. What to do? Do what comes naturally — maintain a separate *rulebook*, as in football. The business process can focus on *a planned response to a business event from beginning to end*; the rulebook can provide the necessary guidance.

> Do what comes naturally — maintain a separate rulebook.

Best Practices

Definitional rules address knowledge; what *people* do is another matter. Having flesh-and-blood people involved 'in the loop' makes a big difference. Best practices in designing business processes with business rules *and people* include:

1. **Avoid mixing definitional and behavioral criteria in the same business rule.** Do people 'in the loop' need to abide by specific results from evaluating definitional rules? If so, specify some behavioral rule(s). For example, classification rules may indicate whether or not an applicant for insurance satisfies all prerequisites. Behavioral rules can indicate whether the decision-maker(s) in the loop *must* accept a qualified applicant — or must *not* accept an *unqualified* applicant.

> Behavioral rules should indicate whether people must abide by results from evaluating definitional rules.

2. **Separate tasks for creating operational knowledge and for people to take business action.** Knowledge-rich tasks (e.g., determining the suitability of an applicant) can be based on definitional rules; the take-action tasks (e.g., hiring the applicant) can be guided by behavioral rules.

> Tasks for creating operational knowledge should be separated from tasks involving business action.

3. **Consider the cost of business rules in developing the business process.** In business terms, it would be *very* costly (if even possible) to gather *all* the data that *any* definitional rule potentially applied in a business process might need. For example, a car insurance company

might have the business rule: *An applicant for car insurance is never considered qualified if the applicant is less than the minimum driving age.* Other business rules might involve creditworthiness (which could involve an extensive credit check), previous driving history (which could require requesting records from the state), and so on. If it can be

determined right from the start the applicant isn't old enough, that's obviously something you want to do. So a basic goal in designing business processes with business rules and people is *work avoidance* (no pun intended). Always test the cheapest rules first wherever possible.

> Avoid unnecessary work in a business process
> by testing cheap rules first.

Summary

A business process model is an end-to-end, results-oriented view of the business tasks appropriate for a planned, optimal response to a significant business event. Business rules capture the decision logic needed for such activity, but do not substitute for the business process itself.

Business process models can be greatly simplified by taking the business rules out and addressing them separately. Benefits include:

- Stable business processes that serve as a framework for managing cross-organizational business activity.

- A new resource, the rulebook, you can use to manage rapid change in business practices.

Chapter 12

Envisioning Really Smart Systems: Dynamic, Thin, Throwaway Procedures

In the National Football League (NFL), if a play is not working for a team, it will be gone from its playbook in short order (possibly along with a coach or two). New plays can be deployed rapidly. In effect, the plays are essentially *throwaways* — cheap enough to discard readily, with minimum disruption or cost. Businesses urgently need something similar — throwaway procedures cheap enough to replace readily when they no longer work well (make 'yardage') for the business.

The reason NFL plays can be treated as throwaways is that the knowledge necessary to run them is embodied elsewhere — in the scoreboard, in the skills of the players, in the heads of the coaches, and most importantly, in the NFL rulebook.

An automated system that can support throwaway procedures would have to be a *smart* system. Business rules would play a major role. This Chapter explains how smart systems would work, taking us to a whole new threshold of software agility.

> Smart systems based on business rules take us
> to a whole new threshold of software agility.

Before we begin, let me clarify something. All definitional rules are automatable; a system that removes evaluation of definitional rules as an application concern (i.e., one that provides a facility for automated reasoning) is already a smart one. That's huge, but let's simply take it as a given. A really smart system is one that also automatically handles flash points and behavioral rules. Read on!

Computational Models for Really Smart Systems

Note to the Reader
At this point, I need to discuss how business-rule-friendly procedures would be designed. If your interest is primarily business rules, you won't miss too much by skipping this section and continuing with the section "Behavioral Rules In Really Smart Systems" on page 134. Be sure not to miss that one though!

In designing a system, you create a computational model (sometimes called a system model). John Zachman notes that a computational model involves

"... surrogates for ... real-world things so that the real-world things can be managed on a scale and at a distance that is not possible in the real world." So, to design smart systems you first need to identify the necessary surrogates.

In the business rules paradigm, the surrogates for real-world business things and how they relate are *facts*. A fact model (structured business vocabulary) is established so you can organize facts massively using real business vocabulary (terms and wordings). For example for the fact type worded *customer places order*, we might have the fact *Global Supply, Inc. has placed the order A601288*.

> Facts are surrogates for real-world business things
> and how they relate.

Facts serve to define state in smart systems. That's the semantic way to define state; any other scheme (e.g., process tokens) is <u>un</u>semantic. Facts, however, basically just sit there until something happens. Something has to happen to stir them up (change state) — you need events. Events can occur:

- Based on execution of some orderly process concocted to do things in a certain way.
- More or less spontaneously, seemingly out of the blue.

Either way (and both are valid), many events that occur are bound to be flash points for business rules. That's where things get really interesting. But let's hold that thought until we develop more groundwork.

What do we mean by *event* in smart systems? We simply mean any change in state — that is, any change in the facts. What kinds of event can happen for a fact? What can you do with one? An order clerk might:

- Request it. For example: *Obtain the credit rating for a customer.*
- Store it. For example: *Store an order placed by a customer.*
- Display it. For example: *Display customer's current account balance.*
- Communicate it. For example: *Insert a special order into a supervisor's work queue for approval.*

Support for the order clerk's system activity would require other kinds of surrogates as well, for example:

- *Work queues.* The supervisor's work queue is actually a *surrogate* for a face-to-face interaction between a supervisor and an order clerk each time a special order is received.
- *Graphical user interfaces (GUIs).* The supervisor's GUI for displaying orders in the queue is actually a *surrogate* for the flesh-and-blood order clerk.

A good name for an orderly process in a computational model is *procedure.* A procedure [MWUD] is simply: *1a: a particular way of doing or of going about the accomplishment of something ... b(3): a series of steps followed in a regular orderly definite way.* The key phrase is *series of steps.*

A procedure is simply a series of steps for manipulating surrogates standing in for real-world things. One thing you won't see in a *smart* procedure is business rules. Now you might see flash points, but that's a different matter. Under Rule Independence, business rules are externalized from procedures into a rulebook. That's how you get *thin* processes.

> You get thin processes by
> externalizing business rules into a rulebook.

A small digression here. If you examine traditional application code closely, you find that only a relatively small portion is actually devoted to the real steps of a procedure. Much of the code is devoted to edits, validations, derivations, and calculations — in other words, to business rules. That's not the end of it. The code also has to detect violations of the behavioral rules in the first place, then map out appropriate responses. So by taking the business rules out, we're talking about *really* thin procedures.

In a smart system, procedures relate to business rules via flash points. Flash points are key to the puzzle. They are how you can create highly *dynamic* procedures — ones that flow dutifully along a series of steps yet that, to an observer, would probably seem *indeterminate*. We still need more groundwork, but you'll see when we get to behavioral rules.

> Highly *dynamic* procedures — ones that seem *indeterminate* —
> result from managing flash points for business rules separately.

Collaboration in Really Smart Systems

A football play is a good analogy for a procedure. A diagram of a football play is literally represented as a collection of orchestrated steps needed to

accomplish the desired result (advance the ball). It's nothing more and nothing less. No business rules — or penalties for violating them — are embedded within it. A play simply focuses on what needs to be done.

A procedure provides a recipe or pattern, a series of steps, for manipulating surrogates. A procedure might be used to take a customer order, evaluate a medical claim, book a reservation, assign a teacher to a class, and so on. Often a procedure is undertaken in response to something that somebody does (e.g., a customer placing an order). A procedure can also be undertaken in response to some timing criteria (e.g., when to bill customers), or to some predefined condition (e.g., inventory quantity on hand is below a certain threshold). In both these latter cases, appropriate criteria for automatically initiating the procedures can be expressed as business rules.

> A procedure provides a recipe or pattern
> for manipulating surrogates.

Series of steps is an apt description of a procedure; *prescribed* series of *requests* is even better.

- By *request* I mean request for action by some surrogate — one of the same kinds of surrogate and action mentioned earlier. Such requests are often (but not always) handled by software components or services presumed to execute. Such software components might include some *factbase management system* (the equivalent of a DBMS except for facts), GUIs, service providers (e.g., print routines), interfaces to legacy systems, work queues, special-purpose business rule analyzers, constraint solvers, and so on.

- By *prescribed* I mean that the series of steps *can* be followed to achieve the desired results, *not* that they must be. For example, there might be one or more other series of steps (procedures) you can follow to achieve the same results. Or if you really know your stuff (think great chefs of Paris), you might achieve the results more or less ad hoc (sparking 'spontaneous' events seemingly out of the blue). To say *must be followed* would represent a business rule about sequencing. It's better to handle such matters by expressing business rules placing restrictions on states (e.g., required antecedents).

People in Really Smart Systems

In many respects, the most important originators or recipients of requests in procedures are people. People, after all, still do a lot of actual work! These people might be either *inside* the company (that is, workers) or *outside* the company (e.g., customers). Although these people might be seen as 'users', we like *actor* better. Here's why. The term *user* suggests outside beneficiaries of system services, whose own work and interactions are outside scope. *Actor*, in contrast, suggests someone whose own activity or role is integral to understanding and doing the work. An actor is someone whose own work is definitely *within* scope.

We do have to be careful here. We're not talking about putting *actual* actors into procedures — that is, real live flesh-and-blood people. You can't put real people into an automated system! Instead, we're actually talking about surrogates that stand in for the actors. Generally these surrogates would be specified as roles (the people kind), but for specific people, they could also be communication links.

> A procedure involves people too.

What can human actors do to move work along in procedures? Two things: (a) perform actions — manually or otherwise — and (b) make requests for action to software components or to other actors.

Here then is the emerging vision for orchestrating work in smart systems — many kinds of actors, some human and some software, collaborating according to really thin, throwaway procedures. By the way, because of the prominent place of human actors in all this, we call (smart) procedures *scripts*. After all, a procedure essentially *scripts* work for a bunch of actors. But for this discussion, I'll stick to *procedure*.

> A procedure prescribes a scripted collaboration
> involving both people and software.

Behavioral Rules in Really Smart Systems

Now we get to the good stuff. To prepare a behavioral rule for its role in smart systems, you need to determine:

1. *What level of enforcement you want for it.* Possible levels of enforcement for behavioral rules and their implications for designing procedures are given in Table 12–1.

2. *How (if at all) you want to react to a violation of it.* Appropriate reactions to violations of a behavioral rule can be given by: (a) some other business rule(s), (b) some procedure(s), or (c) both. These other business rule(s) generally prescribe appropriate sanction(s); the procedures(s) generally layout appropriate response(s).

> Plan responses to violations of a behavioral rule
> as additional business rules or procedures.

Table 12–1. Levels of Enforcement for Behavioral Rules and Their Implications for Designing Procedures.

Level of Enforcement	Description	Implication for Designing Procedures
strictly enforced	If an actor violates the behavioral rule, the actor cannot escape sanction(s).	When a violation is detected, the event producing the violation is automatically prevented, if possible, and a designated violation response, if any, is invoked automatically.
deferred enforcement	The behavioral rule is strictly enforced, but such enforcement may be delayed — e.g., until another actor with required skills and proper authorization can become involved.	When a violation is detected, the event producing the violation is allowed, and the relevant work is handed off to another worker (possibly by insertion into a work queue). Additional business rules giving timing criteria may be desirable to ensure that action is taken within an appropriate timeframe.
override by pre-authorized actor	The behavioral rule is enforced, but an actor with proper before-the-fact authorization may override it.	When a violation is detected, if the actor involved is pre-authorized, that actor is given an opportunity to override the rule. Overrides by actor and business rule should be tracked for subsequent review.
override with real-time waiver	The behavioral rule is enforced, but an actor may request a real-time waiver from another actor having before-the-fact authorization to give such waivers.	When a violation is detected, the actor involved is given an opportunity to interactively request a waiver from a duly-authorized actor. Additional business rules giving timing criteria may be desirable to ensure that some action is taken within an appropriate timeframe. Waivers should be tracked by actor and business rule for subsequent review.
post-justified override	The behavioral rule may be overridden by an actor who is not explicitly authorized; however, if the override is subsequently deemed inappropriate, the actor may be subject to sanction(s).	When an override of a violation occurs, a review item (with all relevant details) should be inserted into the work queue of an appropriate actor for review and possible action.
override with explanation	The behavioral rule may be overridden simply by providing an explanation.	When a violation is detected, the actor involved is given an opportunity to override the business rule by providing a mandatory explanation. Overrides should be tracked by actor and business rule for subsequent review.
guideline	Suggested, but not enforced.	When a violation is detected, the actor involved (if authorized) is simply informed/reminded of the behavioral rule.

About Sleepers
Not included in Table 12–1 is 'not evaluated'. But that's not a level of enforcement; it could also apply to definitional rules. I call a business rule specified not to be evaluated a *sleeper*. A sleeper might literally be just for show (public consumption); more likely, it is not being evaluated because it is pending or retired; deemed inapplicable or overly expensive; etc.

If a behavioral rule is not automatable, you also need to determine how to detect violations. To illustrate, let's work through an example — the offside rule in the game of football: *A player must not be offside.* (Some definitional rule(s) would probably be needed for *offside*, but let's ignore that here.)

1. *What level of enforcement do you want for the offside rule?* Let's say *strictly enforced.*

2. *How (if at all) do you want to react to a violation of the offside rule?* You need another business rule prescribing the appropriate sanction: *The offside team in a play must be penalized five yards or half the distance to the team's own goal line, whichever is less.* We also have a special procedure: *Pace off yardage penalized.*

3. *How will you detect violations of the offside rule?* Since the offside rule is not automatable, detection is assigned to the line judge as a job responsibility. *The line judge watches the play, blows a whistle, throws a flag, stops the play, etc.*

Automatic Flash Points

If the behavioral rule *is* automatable (and a very great many are), that's wonderful news. In a really smart system, you can assume there is an execution-time software platform or service that knows about all flash points and can detect them automatically. Call it the *flash-point service.* Nothing at all needs to be scripted in procedures for detection of violations! The hidden hand of the flash-point service makes procedures *intrinsically* smart.

A really smart system relies on a flash-point service
to automatically detect violations of behavioral rules.

Let's illustrate a smart procedure first with a really dumb scenario:

- We have the behavioral rule: *An order must have a ship-to address.*
- We decide we want the business rule to be *strictly enforced.*
- We do not specify any special response or recourse for a violation.

Now we watch what happens when the (barely) smart procedure executes:

1. A worker initiates the procedure: *Take customer order.*

2. The worker's activity produces an event: *An order is created.*

3. The flash-point service checks whether the event is a flash point. The flash-point service determines that the event is a flash point for the behavioral rule: *An order must have a ship-to address.*

4. The flash-point service checks whether the worker has actually given a ship-to address with the order.

5. Suppose the worker has not done so. The flash-point service causes the event to be rejected — that is, the action (request) fails and the order is not created.

At their strictest, behavioral rules are very narrow-minded. Either the actor plays by the rules, or the work is not accepted. If any question about the quality of the work arises — that is, about its correctness or consistency — the work is simply rejected. In other words, straight-laced behavioral rules *insist* upon the highest quality and do so by active, real-time intervention in ongoing work. Such *real-time compliance* is a distinctive feature of really smart systems under the business rules paradigm.

> Real-time compliance is inherent in really smart systems.

On the other hand, that procedure was almost laughably unfriendly. I call a behavioral rule set up to be strictly enforced without any recourse a *meany.* Generally, that's not going to be a best practice — *unless* the violation represents attempted fraud, theft, or attack. Then 'meanness' (and perhaps appropriate countermeasures) is exactly the right response(!).

But let's suppose the violation is an innocent one. If the worker is authorized and capable, the flash-point service should at the very least present the guidance message (the business rule statement) to the worker. It thereby informs (enlightens) the worker about the business practice, so the worker can correct the problem (by giving a *ship-to-address*) and avoid it in the future. Can a smart procedure be even friendlier? *Of course!* That brings us to re-use.

Flash-Point Re-Use

For smart procedures you want much more than simple re-use through everyday modular design. (Refer to the sidebar.) Re-use of software is good; re-use of procedures based on behavioral rules is *really smart*.

Everyday Modular Design in Procedures

Re-use based on modular design occurs when one procedure simply uses (requests) some other procedure to do a step of its own work. Since the second procedure is not embedded within the first, the second can be requested (re-used) by *other* procedures as well. For example, the procedure *Fill out address* could be potentially (re)used by the procedures: *Take customer order*, *Record prospect information*, *Create shipment*, *Hire employee*, and so on. This kind of reuse is desirable, but involves no special use of business rules.

Specifically, you want *flash-point re-use* of procedures. The mechanics of flash-point re-use work like this:

1. A procedure for undertaking work in normal circumstances is invoked as the designated response to the violation of a behavioral rule.

2. That procedure kicks off automatically whenever a violation of the behavioral rule is detected.

3. If the actor elects to follow through with this second procedure, it steps the actor through correction of the problem. Once resolved, the actor can move on with the original work as scripted by the first procedure.

> Really smart systems support flash-point re-use
> of procedures based on behavioral rules.

The net result of flash-point re-use is a truly *dynamic* work environment, one where procedures are stitched together automatically just-in-time based on what any given actor knows (or doesn't) about current business practices. To an outside observer, the resulting work environment would probably *seem* indeterminate. But that's just the grand illusion of really smart systems.

Table 12–2 illustrates flash-point re-use, step-by-step, for this simple scenario:

Procedure: *Take customer order.*
This procedure is performed by an order entry clerk.

Behavioral Rule: *A customer who places an order over $1,000 must hold an account.*

Violation Response: Invoke the procedure *Establish customer account.* Let's say this is the script normally used to set up accounts, so there's a good chance it would be already familiar to the order entry clerk.

> A work environment that seems indeterminate
> is the grand illusion of really smart systems.

Specifying Violation Responses

A flash-point service for really smart systems would support context-sensitive violation responses for each behavioral rule, as needed. For example, the violation response given in the illustration for the behavioral rule might be selectively specified for:

- A particular procedure.
- A particular flash point.
- A particular flash point in a particular procedure.
- A given class of actor.
- An individual actor.
- etc.

Table 12–1. Levels of Enforcement for Behavioral Rules and Their Implications for Designing Procedures.

Level of Enforcement	Description	Implication for Designing Procedures
strictly enforced	If an actor violates the behavioral rule, the actor cannot escape sanction(s).	When a violation is detected, the event producing the violation is automatically prevented, if possible, and a designated violation response, if any, is invoked automatically.
deferred enforcement	The behavioral rule is strictly enforced, but such enforcement may be delayed — e.g., until another actor with required skills and proper authorization can become involved.	When a violation is detected, the event producing the violation is allowed, and the relevant work is handed off to another worker (possibly by insertion into a work queue). Additional business rules giving timing criteria may be desirable to ensure that action is taken within an appropriate timeframe.
override by pre-authorized actor	The behavioral rule is enforced, but an actor with proper before-the-fact authorization may override it.	When a violation is detected, if the actor involved is pre-authorized, that actor is given an opportunity to override the rule. Overrides by actor and business rule should be tracked for subsequent review.
override with real-time waiver	The behavioral rule is enforced, but an actor may request a real-time waiver from another actor having before-the-fact authorization to give such waivers.	When a violation is detected, the actor involved is given an opportunity to interactively request a waiver from a duly-authorized actor. Additional business rules giving timing criteria may be desirable to ensure that some action is taken within an appropriate timeframe. Waivers should be tracked by actor and business rule for subsequent review.
post-justified override	The behavioral rule may be overridden by an actor who is not explicitly authorized; however, if the override is subsequently deemed inappropriate, the actor may be subject to sanction(s).	When an override of a violation occurs, a review item (with all relevant details) should be inserted into the work queue of an appropriate actor for review and possible action.
override with explanation	The behavioral rule may be overridden simply by providing an explanation.	When a violation is detected, the actor involved is given an opportunity to override the business rule by providing a mandatory explanation. Overrides should be tracked by actor and business rule for subsequent review.
guideline	Suggested, but not enforced.	When a violation is detected, the actor involved (if authorized) is simply informed/reminded of the behavioral rule.

Summary

Let's take one last, hard look at *agility*. Generally, the more *granular* the specifications for a system, the more *adaptable* it will be. Specifications in the business rules paradigm are *highly* granular in these ways:

- Each business rule is specified independently of processes.

- Each business rule is generally specified independently of events.

- Each violation response for a behavioral rule is generally specified independently of procedures.

- The level of enforcement for a behavioral rule is specified independently of the rule itself, and generally independently of events and procedures.

In really smart systems, the flash-point service for behavioral rules is the hidden hand for dynamic, thin, throwaway procedures.

> Specifications in really smart systems are highly granular, yielding true software agility.

Business Rules Manifesto
The Principles of Rule Independence
by Business Rules Group[1]

Article 1. Primary Requirements, Not Secondary
1.1. Rules are a first-class citizen of the requirements world.
1.2. Rules are essential for, and a discrete part of, business models and technology models.

Article 2. Separate From Processes, Not Contained In Them
2.1. Rules are explicit constraints on behavior and/or provide support to behavior.
2.2. Rules are not process and not procedure. They should not be contained in either of these.
2.3. Rules apply *across* processes and procedures. There should be one cohesive body of rules, enforced consistently across all relevant areas of business activity.

Article 3. Deliberate Knowledge, Not A By-Product
3.1. Rules build on facts, and facts build on concepts as expressed by terms.
3.2. Terms express business concepts; facts make assertions about these concepts; rules constrain and support these facts.
3.3. Rules must be explicit. No rule is ever assumed about any concept or fact.
3.4. Rules are basic to what the business knows about itself — that is, to basic business knowledge.
3.5. Rules need to be nurtured, protected, and managed.

Article 4. Declarative, Not Procedural
4.1. Rules should be expressed declaratively in natural-language sentences for the business audience.
4.2. If something cannot be expressed, then it is not a rule.
4.3. A set of statements is declarative only if the set has no implicit sequencing.
4.4. Any statements of rules that require constructs other than terms and facts imply assumptions about a system implementation.
4.5. A rule is distinct from any enforcement defined for it. A rule and its enforcement are separate concerns.
4.6. Rules should be defined independently of responsibility for the *who*, *where*, *when*, or *how* of their enforcement.
4.7. Exceptions to rules are expressed by other rules.

Article 5. Well-Formed Expression, Not Ad Hoc
5.1. Business rules should be expressed in such a way that they can be validated for correctness by business people.
5.2. Business rules should be expressed in such a way that they can be verified against each other for consistency.

5.3.　Formal logics, such as predicate logic, are fundamental to well-formed expression of rules in business terms, as well as to the technologies that implement business rules.

Article 6.　Rule-Based Architecture, Not Indirect Implementation

6.1.　A business rules application is intentionally built to accommodate continuous change in business rules.　The platform on which the application runs should support such continuous change.

6.2.　Executing rules directly — for example in a rules engine — is a better implementation strategy than transcribing the rules into some procedural form.

6.3.　A business rule system must always be able to explain the reasoning by which it arrives at conclusions or takes action.

6.4.　Rules are based on truth values.　How a rule's truth value is determined or maintained is hidden from users.

6.5.　The relationship between events and rules is generally many-to-many.

Article 7.　Rule-Guided Processes, Not Exception-Based Programming

7.1.　Rules define the boundary between acceptable and unacceptable business activity.

7.2.　Rules often require special or selective handling of detected violations.　Such rule violation activity is activity like any other activity.

7.3.　To ensure maximum consistency and reusability, the handling of unacceptable business activity should be separable from the handling of acceptable business activity.

Article 8.　For the Sake of the Business, Not Technology

8.1.　Rules are about business practice and guidance; therefore, rules are motivated by business goals and objectives and are shaped by various influences.

8.2.　Rules always cost the business something.

8.3.　The cost of rule enforcement must be balanced against business risks, and against business opportunities that might otherwise be lost.

8.4.　'More rules' is not better.　Usually fewer 'good rules' is better.

8.5.　An effective system can be based on a small number of rules.　Additional, more discriminating rules can be subsequently added, so that over time the system becomes smarter.

Article 9.　Of, By, and For Business People, Not IT People

9.1.　Rules should arise from knowledgeable business people.

9.2.　Business people should have tools available to help them formulate, validate, and manage rules.

9.3.　Business people should have tools available to help them verify business rules against each other for consistency.

Article 10.　Managing Business Logic, Not Hardware/Software Platforms

10.1.　Business rules are a vital business asset.

10.2.　In the long run, rules are more important to the business than hardware / software platforms.

10.3.　Business rules should be organized and stored in such a way that they can be readily redeployed to new hardware/software platforms.

10.4.　Rules, and the ability to change them effectively, are fundamental to improving business adaptability.

Glossary

Reference Sources
[MWUD]   *Merriam-Webster Unabridged Dictionary* (Version 2.5). [2000]. Merriam-Webster Inc.
[SBVR]   *Semantics of Business Vocabulary and Business Rules (SBVR)*. [January 2008]. Object Management Group.

advice: [SBVR] *a piece of guidance that something is permissible or possible, that there is no rule against it*

assortment: *see* **classification**

behavioral rule: [SBVR] *a business rule that there is an obligation concerning conduct, action, practice, or procedure*

binary fact type: *a fact type that involves exactly two noun concepts*

business event: *an event requiring the business to respond, usually in a non-trivial way and often following some pattern of activity developed in advance, for example, a business process model*

business governance: *a process, organizational function, set of techniques, and systematic approach for creating and deploying policy and business rules into day-to-day business operations*

business policy: *a piece of guidance given for business governance that is not practicable*

business rule: [SBVR] *a rule that is under business jurisdiction*

business vocabulary: *see* **structured business vocabulary**

categorization: *a special element of structure in which one class of things is a category of some other class of things*

categorization scheme: *a scheme used to categorize things into two or more categories (e.g., 'gender' is the scheme for categorizing people as 'male' and 'female')*

category: *a class of things whose meaning is more restrictive, but otherwise compliant with, some other class of things (e.g., person and organization are categories of party)*

classification: *a special element of structure in which a thing is an instance of a class of things*

composition: *see* **whole–part structure**

concept: [MWUD] *something conceived in the mind* : *THOUGHT, IDEA, NOTION*

definition: [MWUD] 2: *a word or phrase expressing the essential nature of a person or thing or class of persons or of things* : *an answer to the question "what is x?" or "what is an x?"*

definitional rule: [SBVR] *a rule that is intended as a definitional criterion*

element of guidance: *a business policy, business rule, or an advice*

elementary fact type: *a fact type that cannot be broken down into two or more other fact types, each with fewer noun concepts, without losing knowledge*

event: [MWUD] 1a(1): *something that happens*

fact model: *the semantic blueprint of a structured business vocabulary*

fact type: *something specific that can be known about one or more noun concepts(s) important to business operations (e.g., that a customer can place an order)*

fact type form: [SBVR] *see* **wording**

flash point: *an event when a business rule needs to be evaluated*

flash-point service: *an execution-time software platform or service that knows about all flash points and can detect them automatically*

GBRS: *see* **general rulebook system**

general rulebook system (GBRS): *an automated, specialized, business-level platform for managing business rules and business vocabulary*

governance: *see* **business governance**

governance process: *a series of actions and checkpoints (i.e., a workflow) indicating who should be doing what, and when, with respect to deploying policy and business rules*

governing rule: *any law, act, statute, regulation, contract, business policy, legal determination, etc., from which business rules can be interpreted*

guidance message: *a rule statement given at a point of knowledge*

know-how: [MWUD] ... *accumulated practical skill or expertness ... especially: technical knowledge, ability, skill, or expertness of this sort*

meany: *a behavioral rule whose enforcement level indicates strict rejection of violations without recourse*

n-ary fact type: *a fact type that involves more than two noun concepts*

nominalization: [MWUD] *the process or result of forming a noun or noun phrase from a clause or a verb*

noun concept: *the concept that a term represents*

objectify: *to cause a fact type (verb concept) to become or to assume the character of a noun concept (e.g., the fact type* 'student enrolls in course offering' *could be objectified as* 'enrollment')

objectification: *the noun concept that results from objectifying a fact type*

operative rule: [SBVR] *see* **behavioral rule**

partitive structure: *see* **whole–part structure**

practicable: *guidance that is ready to deploy into business operations such that it can satisfy the following test: a person who knows about the guidance and who understands the business vocabulary could observe a relevant situation including his or her own behavior and decide directly whether or not the business was complying with the business rule or using it properly*

POK: *see* **point of knowledge**

point of knowledge: *any point where guidance or the company's specialized know-how — i.e., some business rule(s) — is developed, applied, assessed, or retired*

property: [MWUD] 1a: *a quality or trait belonging to a person or thing*

role: *a noun concept that reflects how another noun concept is viewed in context, e.g., in a fact type (for example,* 'owner' *is how* 'person' *is viewed in the fact type worded* 'person [owner] owns vehicle'*)*

rule: [MWUD 'rule'] 1a: *guide for conduct or action* 1f: *one of a set of usually official regulations by which an activity (as a sport) is governed [e.g.,] *the infield fly rule* *the rules of professional basketball** [MWUD 'criteria'] 2: *a standard on which a decision or judgment may be based*

Rule Independence: *the externalization, unification, and management of rules separately from processes*

rulebook: *the collection of business rules for a business, along with the statements, terms, definitions, and wordings that support them*

rulebook management: *the skills, techniques, and processes needed to express, analyze, trace, retain, and manage the decision logic used in day-to-day business operations*

sleeper: *a business rule not to be evaluated (i.e., inactive)*

structural rule: [SBVR] *see* **definitional rule**

structured business vocabulary: *the set of terms and their definitions, and all wordings, that organize operational business knowledge*

term: [MWUD] 8a: *a word or expression that has a precisely-limited meaning in some uses or is peculiar to a science, art, profession, trade, or special subject*

unary fact type: *a fact type that involves exactly one noun concept*

whole–part structure: *a special collection of one or more binary fact types that together describe how a thing of one class of things (the whole) is composed of things of (typically) two or more other classes of things (the parts)*

wording: *an expression including one or more terms and a verb or verb phrase organized appropriately to represent a fact type (e.g.,* 'customer places order'*)*

verb concept: *see* **fact type**

References

Berry, Daniel M., Erik Kamsties, Michael M. Krieger, and Willenken Loh Stris Lee & Tran. [November 2003]. *From Contract Drafting to Software Specification: Linguistic Sources of Ambiguity: A Handbook*, (Version 1.0). ["Ambiguity Handbook"].
Available at: http://se.uwaterloo.ca/~dberry/

Burlton, Roger T. [2001]. *Business Process Management: Profiting from Success*. Indianapolis, IN: Sams Publishing.

Business Rules Group. [September 2007]. *The Business Motivation Model ~ Business Governance in a Volatile World*, (Ver. 1.3).
Available at: http://www.BusinessRulesGroup.org
Note: An adopted standard of the Object Management Group (OMG).

Business Rules Group. [2003]. *Business Rules Manifesto ~ The Principles of Rule Independence*, (Ver. 1.2).
Available at: http://www.BusinessRulesGroup.org
Note: In English as well as more than a dozen other languages.

Business Rules Group. [July 2000]. *Defining Business Rules ~ What Are They Really?* (4th ed).
Available at: http://www.BusinessRulesGroup.org
Note: Formerly known as the *GUIDE Business Rules Project Report*, (1995).

Crystal, David. [2005]. *How Languages Work*. Woodstock, NY: The Overlook Press, Peter Mayer Publishers, Inc.

Editors of BRCommunity.com. [November 2008]. "A Brief History of the Business Rule Approach," *Business Rules Journal*, Vol. 9, No. 11.
Available at: http://www.BRCommunity.com/a2008/b448.html

Halpin, Terry (with Tony Morgan). [2008]. *Information Modeling and Relational Databases*, (2nd Ed.), San Francisco, CA: Morgan Kaufmann.

ISO 1087-1. [2000]. *Terminology Work — Vocabulary, Part 1: Theory and Application*.

ISO 704. [2000]. *Terminology Work — Principles and Methods*.

Lam. Gladys S. W. [May/June 1998]. "Business Knowledge — Packaged in a Policy Charter," *DataToKnowledge Newsletter*, Vol. 26, No. 3.
Available at: http://www.BRCommunity.com/a1998/a385.html

Merriam-Webster Unabridged Dictionary, (Version 2.5). [2000]. Merriam-Webster Inc.

Nijssen, Sjir. [July 1981]. *An Architecture for Knowledge Base Software*. Presented at the Australian Computer Society conference. Available at: http://www.FBMf.eu

Pinker, Steven. [2007]. *The Stuff of Thought: Language as a Window into Human Nature*. New York, NY: Viking.

Ross, Ronald G. [1994, 1997]. *The Business Rule Book*. Business Rule Solutions, LLC.

Ross, Ronald G. [2003]. *Principles of the Business Rule Approach*. Boston, MA: Addison-Wesley.

Ross, Ronald G. [July 2007]. "What's Wrong with If-Then Syntax For Expressing Business Rules ~ One Size Doesn't Fit All," *Business Rules Journal*, Vol. 8, No. 7. Available at: http://www.BRCommunity.com/a2007/b353.html

Ross, Ronald G. [March 2008]. "The Emergence of SBVR and the True Meaning of 'Semantics': Why You Should Care (a Lot!) ~ Part 1," *Business Rules Journal*, Vol. 9, No. 3. Available at: http://www.BRCommunity.com/a2008/b401.html

Semantics of Business Vocabulary and Business Rules (SBVR), (Version 1.0). [January 2008]. Object Management Group. Available at: http://www.omg.org/spec/SBVR/1.0/

Taylor, James and Neil Raden. [2007]. *Smart (Enough) Systems*. Boston, MA: Prentice-Hall.

Index

A

accelerating rate of change, 120-122

Accommodation, 95-96

accountability, 36, 39, 42

actors, 133-134, 135, 137-140

advices (non-rules), 84, 92-93

agility
business, 42, 122
business rules in achieving, 104, 118, 120
granularity in achieving, 105, 141
single-sourcing of business rules in
achieving, 24, 104
throwaway procedures in achieving, 129
of software, 129-140, 141

always, 89

ambiguity in business rules, 15, 45

analysis, see *business analysis*

anomalies in business rules, 106, 107-108

architectures, see *smart architectures*

assortments, see *classifications*

automatable vs. non-automatable rules, 85,
87, 129, 136

B

behavioral rules, 86-88, 90, 125-126, 127,
129, 134-140

binary fact types, 69, 70

Burlton, Roger, 123, 124, 125

business agility, 42, 122

business analysis
and business process models, 125, 127-128
and business rule quality, 37, 106-108, 110
and business rules, 28-29, 103-104, 127-128
and business vocabulary, 21-22
and fact models, 54

business communication
avoiding ambiguity in, 15, 46
and business vocabulary, 13, 14, 17-18, 20
challenge of, 54
clarity of, 51-53
and fact models, 59
forms of, 12
formal vs. conversational, 95-97
of knowledge, 11, 15
and requirements, 54
and structural models, 51-53
support for, 20, 46-48, 92

business governance, 37-42

Business Motivation Model, 41

business processes
behavioral rules in, 88, 125-126, 127
best practices for business rules, 125, 127-28
and business rules, 29-30, 57-58, 123-128
and decisioning, 124-125
definition of, 123
definitional rules in, 124-125, 127
diamonds in, 125
dynamic, 119, 132, 139
and guidance, 124, 126
and knowledge, 119, 127
managing on the basis of, 123
models of, 123, 124-125
smart, 115, 119
stability in, 123
work avoidance in models of, 128

business policies, 39, 85

business rules management, see *rulebook
management*

business rule quality
completeness, 108, 110, 111-112
overview of, 37, 106-108

business rules
vs. advices (non-rules), 84, 92-93
agility supported by, 104, 118, 120, 122, 141
anomalies in, 106, 107-108
in application code, 131
automatable vs. non-automatable, 85, 87,
129, 136
behavioral, 86-88, 90, 125-126, 127, 129,
134-140
benefits of, 5, 24, 36, 42, 104, 122, 128
vs. business policies, 85
and business governance, 38-39
and business jurisdiction, 83, 87, 89
and business practices, 61-62, 66, 96
and business processes, 29-30, 123-128
and business vocabulary, 13, 15, 26, 86
categorization of, 83, 84-91
classification by, 89-90, 124
in compliance, 126, 137
computation by, 90
conflicts in, 95-97, 107
cost of, 32, 127-128
and CRUD events, 102-104
and data quality, 33
vs. data rules, 52, 102
decision logic in the form of, 90
decision tables used to represent, 108-112

C

About the Author
Ronald G. Ross

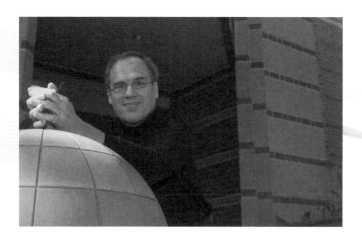

Ronald G. Ross is recognized internationally as the "father of business rules." He serves as Executive Editor of Business Rules Community (www.BRCommunity.com) and its flagship publication, *Business Rules Journal*. He is a sought-after speaker at conferences world-wide. More than 50,000 people have heard him speak; many more than that have read his books. His popular public seminars are given through AttainingEdge and in Europe though IRM-UK.

Mr. Ross has served as Chair of the annual International Business Rules Forum Conference since 1997. He was a charter member of the Business Rules Group (BRG) in the 1980s, and an editor of the two landmark BRG papers, "The Business Motivation Model: *Business Governance in a Volatile World*" and the "Business Rules Manifesto." He is active in OMG standards development, with core involvement in SBVR.

Mr. Ross is the author of eight professional books, including the ground-breaking, first book on business rules *The Business Rule Book* (1994) and *Principles of the Business Rule Approach*, Addison-Wesley (2003). He holds a BA from Rice University and an MS in information science from IIT.

For more information about Mr. Ross, visit www.RonRoss.info.

About ...

 Business Rule Solutions, LLC

Business Rule Solutions, LLC — Business Rule Solutions, LLC is the recognized world leader in the advancement of business rules and decisioning. Co-founders Ronald G. Ross and Gladys S.W. Lam are internationally acclaimed as the foremost experts and practitioners of business rule techniques and methodology.

Since its inception in 1996, BRS has helped pilot the worldwide growth of business rules. BRS offers Proteus®, its landmark business analysis and business rules methodology, including the popular *RuleSpeak®*. Services include consulting, training, and presentations. For more information about BRS, visit www.BRSolutions.com.

BRCommunity.com

BRCommunity — Business Rules Community is a vertical, non-commercial community for decisioning and business rule professionals, providing articles, expert commentary, panels, and a variety of other hands-on resources. BRCommunity.com and its flagship publication, the Business Rules Journal, were established in 2000. Visit www.BRCommunity.com.